PRINCE

PRINCE
THE LAST INTERVIEW
and OTHER CONVERSATIONS

with an introduction by HANIF ABDURRAQIB

MELVILLE HOUSE
BROOKLYN · LONDON

PRINCE: THE LAST INTERVIEW AND OTHER CONVERSATIONS

"Nelson finds it 'hard to become known'" by Lisa Crawford was first published in February 1976 by the *Central High Pioneer*, a student journal published by the Minneapolis Central High School.

"Prince" by Lisa Hendricksson (April 8, 1977) was reprinted with permission of *The Minnesota Daily*.

"A Dirty Mind Comes Clean" by Andy Schwartz, first published in the *New York Rocker* in June 1981, was reprinted with permission of Rock's Backpages.

"Prince's First Ever Interview for Television" originally aired November 15, 1985. MTV's "1985 Prince Interview" used with permission by MTV. © 2018 Viacom Media Networks. All Rights Reserved. MTV, all related titles, characters and logos are trademarks owned by Viacom Media Networks, a division of Viacom International Inc.

"Pleased to Meet You . . ." by Adrian Deevoy, first published in *Q Magazine* (#94) in July 1994, was reprinted with permission of Rock's Backpages.

"A Prince of a Guy" by Catherine Censor Shemo, first published in *Vegetarian Times* in October 1997, was reprinted with permission of *Clean Eating* and *Vegetarian Times*.

"Sites O' the Times" © 1997 by Ben Greenman was first published in *Yahoo! Internet Life* in October 1997.

"Soup with Prince" by Claire Hoffman, first published in *The New Yorker* on November 24, 2008, was reprinted with permission of Condé Nast Inc.

"A Final Visit with Prince: Rolling Stone's Lost Cover Story" by Brian Hiatt, first published in *Rolling Stone* on May 2, 2016. Copyright © 2016 by *Rolling Stone* LLC.

"'Transcendence. That's What You Want. When That Happens—Oh, Boy'" by Alexis Petridis, first published in *The Guardian* on November 12, 2015, was reprinted with permission of *Guardian* News and Media Ltd 2018. All rights reserved. Used by permission.

Every reasonable effort has been made to trace the owners of the copyright for "Nelson finds it 'hard to become known,'" but this has proved impossible. The publishers and editors will be glad to receive any information leading to more complete acknowledgments for subsequent printings of this book.

The publisher thanks Christina Cerio for her editorial assistance on this book—it would not have happened without her.

Melville House Publishing
46 John Street
Brooklyn, NY 11201

and

Melville House UK
Suite 2000 16/18 Woodford Rd
London E7 0H2

mhpbooks.com
@melvillehouse

ISBN: 978-1-61219-745-6
ISBN: 978-1-61219-746-3 (eBook)

Printed in the United States of America

10 9 8 7 6 5 4 3 2 1

A catalog record for this book is available from the Library of Congress.

CONTENTS

INTRODUCTION

HANIF ABDURRAQIB

Like so many other American kids of the late 1980s and early '90s, I stumbled my way to musical consciousness during a time when music had become very self-conscious and, rather than feel otherworldly, I was listening to music that sounded like it was being made by regular people.

That changed when I was eight years old. At a friend's house, I discovered a copy of Prince's *Dirty Mind*, the cover of which features a photo of Prince in nothing more than a leather jacket and underwear, adorned only by a bandanna slung across his bare chest. It had a strange power: when my friend's mother saw the album in my hands, my eyes

magnetized by Prince's image, she scolded me and took it
away.

But Prince was unavoidable and provocative, someone
who looked regal sitting on a purple motorcycle, his back
haloed with smoke; someone who could dance with his ass
out on television whether the parents of young viewers liked
it or not. That the sight alone of this person could allure and
frighten, that he seemed to exist outside of the streets of hip-
hop and the suburbs of grunge, that's how I came to fall in
love with Prince and what he stood for.

Dirty Mind had been released before I was born, and my
generation would not inherit Prince the sex symbol. Instead
we were given Prince the literal symbolist—in an era when
Prince replaced ostentatious lyricism with hermetic gestures
toward ideas—both musical ideas and ideas of the self. He
was "The Artist Formerly Known as Prince," and then "The
Artist," and then "The Gifted One," and then just "⚦" a
glyph that could not be spoken out loud.

To call a musician ahead of his or her time is an oft-
used phrase that—far too commonly—gets attached to some
mundane or uneventful exercise: a suggestive lyric here, or
a music video there. For Prince, to be ahead of one's time
meant to have an active hand in both shaping music—how
it would be heard, how it would be interpreted, how it would
be distributed—for generations to come.

In 1996, around the time that Prince released *Emancipation*—
a three-disc, two-and-a-half-hour album—I embarked on
a quest to "figure out" why Prince no longer wanted to be

Prince. Even though by this time I was old enough to buy his albums for myself, this was surely a rash undertaking on my part. The year 1996 had been one of Prince's most prolific—along with Emancipation there had been another album (*Chaos and Disorder*) as well as a soundtrack to the Spike Lee film *Girl 6*. You would not be able to define Prince by this material; instead, what you are given is a display of his superhuman capacity to hold so many other people inside of himself—the sexual Prince, the ambitious Prince, the political Prince, the historical Prince—and his ability to satisfy each of their sonic and aesthetic needs. Simply put, I ended up grasping at a multifaceted figure.

I didn't know it at the time, but *Emancipation* was the first work Prince released after he shook himself free of his Warner Bros. contract. Hence the title, hence the ⚥ and a pair of unshackled hands on the cover. I remember expecting an album as good as *Purple Rain* or *Dirty Mind*, but instead found the album uneven. It had the creative excitement and optimism of an artist tapping into an unbound imagination. I even recall pulling out the scroll of liner notes and finding every usage of the pronoun "I" replaced by a drawing of an "eye" symbol. But it challenged the very notion of curation. Warner Bros. didn't want to control the artist, I would later realize, they wanted to filter his output. And it was that difference and its implications that made my quest that much more difficult.

One thing I did not have to aid me were words from Prince himself. He was a notoriously guarded interviewee, sometimes offering nothing more than a "yes" or "no" to an interviewer's question. This stance goes back to even his earliest interviews.

While happily conversant for a 1976 interview with his high
school paper, only a year later, in an interview for the *Minnesota Daily*, a reticent eighteen-year-old Prince had emerged.
The interviewer only includes, or is only allowed to include, a
paltry number of quotes. Yet what she takes away is juicy, even
if, as she notes, Prince's impatience at having to sit through an
interview is obvious.

Though Prince could be a difficult interview subject,
I can't help but sympathize with his reasons for being so.
Interviewing at its best is a match between what a speaker
is willing to give and what a listener is willing to take away.
I've been on both sides of that table; I have sympathy for
both speaker and listener. Interviews can fail when there is
an expectation that something large must be revealed: some
long-held truth, finally unraveled for a waiting public. I find
that the best interview—as both speaker and listener—is one
of restraint, where the tools necessary to unearth something
during the more silent moments—patience, a sharp ear, and
a ready pen—are used to bring about some of the best moments of the conversation.

Reading these interviews now is to see just how much
Prince adhered to this type of negotiation. Not included here
are several interviews where Prince barely offered up more
than one-sentence answers, and even in the more substantial
interviews this collection gathers, interviewers clearly had to
work to get Prince into an actual dialogue, sometimes with
wince-inducing results. In an interview for *Q Magazine* in
1994, when pushed on a question about why sex was such a
dominant theme in his work (the interviewer insisted that
"Come," the title track of his then newest album, had to be

about orgasm), Prince responds: "Is it? That's your interpretation? Come where? Come to whom? Come for what? [*laughs*]
That's just the way you see it. It's your mind."

In pugnacious moments like these, Prince is not rude
or combative, but he does make it understood that anyone
speaking to him should work hard to get the good stuff. He
knew he didn't need to answer any question asked of him
or to talk to anyone if he didn't want to. Even when he did,
these conversations could be hard to come by. Back when I
first started my informal study of Prince, the internet was
too young to be useful: you couldn't google "Prince interview" because Google wasn't founded until 1998 (it's worth
noting that Prince, adaptable to changing technologies, had
launched his website nearly a year prior).

Sometime after the dust had settled over his battle with
Warner Bros., Prince became more gregarious. It seemed to
suit his image to make yet another shift, to maneuver the language surrounding him from grandiose and guarded toward
something more intimate and convivial. In a 2008 interview
with *The New Yorker*, Prince tells a story about a woman who
had been lingering on the swings outside of his Paisley Park
residence. He went out to talk to her, telling her that his security suggested that he call the police, but he instead wanted
to know what she wanted. "In the end, all she wanted was
to be seen," he says. "Just for me to look at her. She left and
never came back."

The true gift of these interviews is not finding out some
previously unknown bit of information about Prince, as
much as it is to confirm that he could astound even himself.
That's the trick, I suppose, at being someone like Prince. You

had to stay immersed in the unbelievable to achieve it. In what would be his final published interview, a 2015 conversation with *The Guardian*, Prince tells the interviewer of having a recent "out-of-body experience" playing and singing alone at his home in Paisley Park for three hours straight. "That's what you want," he tells the interviewer. "Transcendence. When that happens . . . oh, boy."

When a musician dies, this thing happens where stories about them overflow and fill every corner of the internet. If there is a bright spot in the absence death leaves, it is this one— people recalling their encounters with figures who could seem entirely mythological. For a lascivious figure, he followed for much of his life (and up to a point) the strict orthodoxy of the Jehovah's Witnesses. No alcohol or drugs; he didn't even swear. On Twitter, Talib Kweli recounted the story about DJing gangsta rap at a party that Prince had attended. He approached Kweli to tell him: "I ain't get dressed up to come out and hear curses."

But he loved to be active and athletic. There was the story Questlove told about Prince on a singular and bright pair of roller skates, outdoing everyone else at the roller rink. He was rumored to be a talented basketball player as well, something which lent Dave Chappelle's famous skit of Prince challenging Charlie Murphy to a game of hoops a bit more gravitas.

And then there were those facts that simply defied logic. Old friends of Prince like Corey Tollefson and Kandace Springs insisted that you could tell Prince was about to enter a room because the smell of lavender would arise. Also mysterious was how, in one performance of "My Guitar Gently Weeps" with Tom Petty for the Rock & Roll Hall of Fame, he finished an astounding solo by throwing his guitar up into the rafters. It never came back down.

The moment that best captured his magic for me occurred during his 2007 Super Bowl halftime show. He played amid a torrential downpour, bouncing on a slick stage shaped in the symbol that once stood in for his name. He ripped through a cover of "Proud Mary" and reinvented "Best Of You" by the Foo Fighters, a song that, by then, was less than two years old. But it was his performance of "Purple Rain," his finale that night, which still gets me. During the guitar solo Prince tears into to close out his signature track, I noticed specks of rainwater marching slowly down Prince's face and kissing his bright blue suit and the orange shirt beneath it. I had watched that performance live with friends and remember joking with them that the water did not appear to be touching him, a confirmation that he was not of this world. But when I rewatched this performance soon after his death, it was only then, so many years later, that I confirmed the water had always been there. Prince was getting rained on just like everyone else packed into that football stadium.

For a lifetime spent first trying to figure Prince out, only to end up attributing an over-imagined lore to him, it was easy for me to detach from the idea that Prince—as mystifying as he managed to be—was also very human. It was there in his music, his visuals, his passions, and his curiosities—his humanity. And toward the end of his life, it seemed that being human was his biggest shift yet. During a 2014 interview for *Rolling Stone*, Prince tells Brian Hiatt that he is entirely uninterested in talking about the past, despite his past containing, by that point, so many gems worth unearthing and unraveling. "[T]here is no place else I'd rather be than right now," Prince tells Hiatt. "I want to be talking to you, and I want you to get it."

This is the joy of Prince—all of him. Not only what is contained within this collection of beautiful, challenging, and brilliant conversations, but the entirety of the life this book is honoring. Prince was spectacular, unfathomable in some ways, yet at his core he came to conversations asking to not be made into some kind of god, demanding any asker of questions to understand him beyond his superhuman capabilities. Before anyone else could, it was Prince who recognized his mortality, could sense it creeping up on him, and accepted it. That's what brought Prince down to earth for me. Even if the adoring public missed it the first time, even if it were easy to deify him—Prince, the man, was always there, pointing to the raindrops on his jacket.

PRINCE

NELSON FINDS IT "HARD TO BECOME KNOWN"

INTERVIEW WITH LISA CRAWFORD
CENTRAL HIGH PIONEER
APRIL 1976

"I play with Grand Central Corporation. I've been playing with them for two years," Prince Nelson, senior at Central, said. Prince started playing piano at age seven and guitar when he got out of eighth grade.

Prince was born in Minneapolis. When asked, he said, "I was born here, unfortunately." Why? "I think it is very hard for a band to make it in this state, even if they're good. Mainly because there aren't any big record companies or studios in this state. I really feel that if we would have lived in Los Angeles or New York or some other big city, we would have gotten over by now."

He likes Central a great deal, because his music teachers let him work on his own. He now is working with Mr. Bickham, a music teacher at Central, but has been working with Mrs. Doepkes.

He plays several instruments, such as guitar, bass, all keyboards, and drums. He also sings sometimes, which he picked up recently. He played saxophone in seventh grade but gave it up. He regrets he did. He quit playing sax when school ended one summer. He never had time to practice sax anymore when he went back to school. He does not play in the school band. Why? "I really don't have time to make the concerts."

Prince has a brother that goes to Central whose name is Duane Nelson, who is more athletically enthusiastic. He plays on the basketball team and played on the football team. Duane is also a senior.

Prince plays by ear. "I've had about two lessons, but they didn't help much. I think you'll always be able to do what your ear tells you, so just think how great you'd be with lessons also," he said.

"I advise anyone who wants to learn guitar to get a teacher unless they are very musically inclined. One should learn all their scales too. That is very important," he continued.

Prince would also like to say that his band is in the process of recording an album containing songs they have composed. It should be released during the early part of the summer.

"Eventually I would like to go to college and start lessons again when I'm much older."

PRINCE

INTERVIEW WITH LISA HENDRICKSSON
MINNESOTA DAILY
APRIL 1977

The American recording industry isn't exactly glutted by musicians from Minneapolis. The few who do make it big internationally, like Leo Kottke and Michael Johnson, are firmly embedded in the acoustic folk tradition that defines the Minneapolis music scene.

With the flowering of the sophisticated, well-equipped Sound80 recording studio, all that may change, however. Acts as diverse as Cat Stevens and KISS have recorded there, and local bands like Lamont Cranston are cutting albums. Clearly, Minneapolis is beginning to break free from its folk-oriented roots.

If he makes it, the most atypical local star to come out of Sound80 will be a multitalented, eighteen-year-old prodigy from North Minneapolis who plays any instrument you hand him, sings with a crystal-pure falsetto that would have put the young Michael Jackson to shame, and goes by the name Prince. No last name, and please, no "the" prefix. Just Prince.

If you haven't heard of him yet, you're not alone, though you may have danced to rough mixes of his songs (without knowing it) at Scotties. Right now, Prince is probably the best-kept musical secret in Minneapolis, known mainly to local session musicians and recording studio habitués. The reason he's not already a well-known local performer is simple: ambition. This kid wants to be a major national recording star, and the way to do that is not to wear out your vocal cords at the Tempo night after night. A smart, anxious eighteen-year-old isn't going to sit still for a lecture about paying dues, either. He's got his program pretty well worked out, and the wheels are in motion. From where he and his manager are sitting, it's only a matter of time.

Prince is making an obvious effort to hide his impatience the night I visited him during a recording session at Sound80 a few weeks back. The WAYL [radio] Strings were trying to lay down a not too difficult track that Prince had written, and the 16th notes were coming out like mush. They plugged away for about an hour when Prince very politely told the conductor to change the 16th notes to quarter notes. This done, he slumped down in his seat, looking dissatisfied and slightly annoyed. "We won't be able to use that. I hate wasting time. I want to hear that song on the radio."

It's a little startling, hearing this from a teenager, albeit an extraordinarily talented and self-possessed teenager. But when you begin playing piano at six, guitar at thirteen, bass soon after, and finally master the drums at fourteen, your time schedule gets pushed forward a bit.

Prince was spotted playing in a high school band by Chris Moon of Moonsound, another, smaller local recording studio. His excellence was immediately apparent, and Moon began collaborating with him in the studio, putting together tapes. With several songs in the can, Prince headed for New Jersey to find fame and fortune by way of Atlantic Records. The people of Atlantic, though impressed, suggested that his sound was "too Midwestern"—whatever that means. Others, notably Tiffany Entertainment, a company owned by basketball player Earl Monroe, made offers which Prince apparently could refuse, because by winter he returned to Minneapolis.

Things got back on the track in December, when Prince's tapes made such a big impression on former Twin Cities promoter Owen Husney that Husney decided to come out of comfortable ad agency anonymity to manage Prince. Together, they've spent the entire winter in Sound80, polishing the production on the three or four songs they intend to present to all the major labels in Los Angeles next week. Husney is confident about Prince's chances for a contract, citing the capriciousness of the record business as the main roadblock. With typical managerial optimism, he says, "If he isn't [signed], it'll be because somebody's wife burned the eggs that morning."

How much basis is there for this optimism? A great deal, I think. For one thing, Prince has two valuable gimmicks going for him—his age and his versatility. Not only does he play every instrument on the Sound80 tapes, he also does all the vocal tracks and has written and arranged all the songs himself. It's a prodigious feat, made all the more impressive by the fact that he's self-taught. Although his father was a jazz musician, Prince insists that he didn't actually teach him anything, nor did they play together very often. He seems to have gotten the ability by osmosis.

Another strong point is the obvious commercial appeal of his sound. It's sweet, funky disco soul, but I'll deemphasize the "disco" because the arrangements are more sophisticated and inventive, less formulaic than the simplistic repetitiveness one associates with disco. His use of a driving synthesizer on one song, "Soft and Wet" is traceable to Stevie Wonder, and his phrasing derives a little from Rufus's Chaka Khan. If he hasn't totally transcended his influences, he certainly has assimilated them convincingly.

The development of this pop sound troubles Prince a little. He has spent his adolescence around good musicians and understands the value of respect. Ideally, he says, he would like to record jazz on one label under a pseudonym and the pop stuff on another label.

Finally, there is Prince's personal appeal. As a performer, he should have little trouble. Not only can he jump from instrument to instrument, but he's the kind of cute that drives the boppers crazy. He's not adverse to choreography, but draws the line at spins. "I get nauseous," he explains.

In an interview situation, he's quiet, even aloof, with a sly sense of humor and a quick, intelligent smile. You get the feeling that not even at gunpoint would this kid make a fool of himself in public. Before I talked to him, his manager assured me he didn't use drugs or alcohol and wouldn't jive with me. I actually believe the former, but not the latter. Jive takes many forms, and this cool eighteen-year-old has it down to a subtle art.

After the recording session everyone went out to Perkins for coffee. Tired of having to act twice his age for the elderly WAYL gang, Prince ordered a milkshake and began adding things to it—ketchup, blueberry syrup, honey, steak sauce, coffee, jam, salt and pepper. He ordered the waitress over to the table and handed her the concoction.

Opening his large brown eyes even wider, he said, "I think there's something wrong with this. It tastes funny." The worried waitress asked what it was supposed to be and hurried over to the manager, who formally apologized and took it off the bill. Prince brought off the whole scene with a royal aplomb befitting of his name.

What a relief. Earlier in the studio, I was sure he was a clone, constructed in the back rooms of Owen Husney's ad agency. Prince is a real live kid, packed with talent, but basically normal and mischievous. Besides his music, that was the nicest surprise of the evening.

A DIRTY MIND COMES CLEAN

INTERVIEW WITH ANDY SCHWARTZ
NEW YORK ROCKER
JUNE 1981

Who is the real Prince, anyway? The flashy, high-energy black pop star with the Stratocaster, wearing Iggy Pop's underwear? Or the pleasant, soft-spoken fellow who slumps in this hotel room armchair in a wrinkled raincoat and a "Rude Boy" button? They're one and the same of course, and they've combined to give us Dirty Mind, *a high-ranking entry among the very best records of 1980, which continues to pick up enthusiastic listeners several months after its initial release.*

You've heard of puppy love? Well, Dirty Mind *is an album of puppy sex. Prince's lilting falsetto can make even the most taboo practices sound like good clean teenage fun, while his simple, carefully crafted rhythm tracks and pulsating guitar lines ebb and flow in endlessly listenable loops of sound. Is Prince the black new wave we've been waiting for? Well. he's part of it . . .*

ANDY SCHWARTZ: I know something about your early bands [see "Prince: Local Color"]. But I'm curious to know how you learned your way around the studio well enough to make these albums all by yourself.

PRINCE: I basically learned with two tape recorders, two cassette recorders. That taught me how to mix harmonies and run harmonies together, to play along with myself.

SCHWARTZ: Did music run in your family?

PRINCE: Well, my father was a musician—he headed up his own big band, playing around the Midwest and stuff, and my mother sang for the band. He left when I was seven, so music left with him. But he did leave his piano, and that's when I started learning how to play.

SCHWARTZ: Was your mother supportive of your musical aspirations?

PRINCE: [*Shakes head "No"*] She wanted me to go to school, go to college—she sent me to a bunch of different schools. I always had a pretty high academic level. I guess . . . She always tried to send me to the best schools, but that was pretty much my second interest. I didn't really care about that as much as I did about playing. I think music is what broke her and my father up, and I don't think she wanted that for me . . . Musicians, depending on how serious they are, they're really moody. Sometimes they need a lotta space, they want everything just right sometimes, y'know. My father was a great deal like that, and my mother didn't give him a lotta space. She wanted a husband per se.

SCHWARTZ: What kind of "space" do you need to make music, to write songs?

PRINCE: It used to be I'd have to be totally isolated to write things, because a lotta things I wrote concerned different visions and dreams and fantasies I had. But lately I have to be around people, I have to see different places and stuff like that. just walk through life, I guess . . .You know, it's interesting—if I try to get myself away from being a musician and just, you know, live life. I can write much better. Different things happen, you run into different relationships . . .

SCHWARTZ: I guess that's why so many performers seem to do their best work at the earliest stage of their careers, before they become "professional musicians" working on a schedule set by the record company and the demands of an audience. Your input changes, your sources change.

PRINCE: That's already true. This last album [*Dirty Mind*], I wasn't even working during the time it was done—I wasn't sure this was what I really wanted to do. When I'm not touring, I like to just hang.

SCHWARTZ: When you have the time, are you a fan of music? Do you listen to a lot of records, buy a lot of records?

PRINCE: No. I just get what Warner Bros. sends me, but I don't listen to very much.

SCHWARTZ: Are there any records of the last few months or year that struck you as particularly exciting or special?

PRINCE: I wish there was, but I guess if there were we wouldn't be in the slump we are in the music business.

SCHWARTZ: Do you think that's the problem? That the music itself isn't bringing people into record stores and concerts the way it once did?

PRINCE: Yeah. I think they're getting hip to the fact that musicians are becoming too business-oriented, too much into the money aspect of it. It's turned so commercial—it's beginning to get like Saran wrap, and people are getting hip to it. And until it gets back to the street, I don't think it's gonna pick up.

SCHWARTZ: Do you think too many musicians are sitting down to write songs purely on the basis of what radio will play and what they think will sell?

PRINCE: Exactly. Owen [Husney, his first manager] used to tell me a lotta times that when he was growing up there weren't really fads, y'know, musical fads, fashion fads, things like that. That when he was coming up, people were trying to do something different from the next cat. I guess that's probably how pyschedelic music came into being. Because everybody was trying to be so out and crazy, it just went overboard. But I think that's the way to be. because it's coming from inside instead of "okay, this is what's happening and I'm gonna do this."

SCHWARTZ: You were seventeen years old, had no band as such, and didn't live in a major music-biz city. How did you get signed?

PRINCE: See, I had originally gone to New York, and I got two offers when I came out here to live with my sister. The only problem there was I didn't have a cat in there fighting for me, to get me artistic control over the production end of it. Owen was convinced that no one could produce a record of mine but me. I don't know whether I really agreed with him at the time, but I know I believed in his gusto, in his belief. I didn't know if I was old enough or smart enough—it sounded like a big term, y'know, "producer" of an album. I didn't know it didn't really mean that much at all.

SCHWARTZ: Do you think the producer is an overrated figure in music today?

PRINCE: Well, a lotta records today are producer's records. To *me* it doesn't mean anything, because I don't believe in any act, really, which has to rely on a producer. What happens if the cat dies? There you go, there goes your sound—you obviously didn't have one. The producer bakes the whole cake . . . and that's probably why I don't listen to music. The artist is singing songs he didn't even write . . .

SCHWARTZ: This tour and this album may change things, but your records and concert tickets are still bought mostly by black people. How do you feel about the restrictions, particularly in radio, on musicians who happen to be black, as opposed to musicians whose sound can be more easily classified as "disco" or "R&B" or "funk"? Like this *Village Voice* article asks, "Will rock stations in 1981 play Prince like they played Jimi Hendrix and Sly Stone in 1971?"

PRINCE: Well, I don't know, music has changed so much since then. It's gotten pretty well segregated now . . . I think it's gonna come from the people, it's gonna be whatever they wanna hear and how much support they put behind what I do. With the jocks coming to check us out—I mean, it's gotta be a matter of taste, not doing it because they did it in 1971, but because they wanna do it and they feel it fits. I can sense the restrictions that come up, as far as our concerts and radio is concerned, but it doesn't really bother me. People are gonna come and see what they want, they'll buy what they want—I don't basically worry about it too much.

The record's not doing phenomenally well sales-wise, and airplay is pretty minimal, so I don't worry about it much. What money is made usually goes back into our stage show and to support everybody. You gotta do what you feel and hope it gets to as many people as it can.

SCHWARTZ: Are you much involved with the business side of things? Do you watch the charts, caff up the promotion men, this kind of thing?

PRINCE: Well, when my first album came out I used to watch the charts, but I gave up on it after that. It became so . . . See, you can look at the charts and you know for a fact that your record is better than some of the things that are over you. But I could look at it objectively and realize why those records were ahead of mine, that it's all basically business politics . . . I just now started to meet some of the radio guys and the promo people. Originally I didn't want to do any of that, because it was basically a stroking game and I didn't want to get involved in it at all. Now that people have seen us, though, I think they're genuinely into it and I don't mind meeting people who really dig us, rather than "Well, this cat gave me a television set so I'm gonna play his jam, and it's been nice meeting you."

SCHWARTZ: How about your own friends and acquaintances at home? Can you perceive a change in the way they relate to you now that you're a "rock star?"

PRINCE: People that know me basically stayed the same—we'll be friends to the end, I guess. People that don't know me— they pop out of everywhere now, all these so-called friends who remember me back in school. A lot of people say that the person who goes through it all changes, but I don't think that's true. I think it's everyone else who changes, because they expect certain things from you and they'll approach you in a different manner. As far as moving is concerned—I can't stand L.A., so I would never move there . . . Every time I have to go out there, I dread it. It's that attitude of everybody—I lose sight of what I'm doing when I'm there, it's like a dream factory . . . They spend so much money! They make it and spend it, and for crazy reasons . . .

SCHWARTZ: You stand to make a lot of money someday. What would you do with it if you had it?

PRINCE: I'd give a lot of it away. Every once in a while now

I get some money that's a little extra, and I just give it away.

SCHWARTZ: To friends, strangers, charity?

PRINCE: Friends, strangers—no charities. I've yet to find one that I really felt strong enough about. But friends, strangers—I just get personal satisfaction out of seeing people happy.

SCHWARTZ: We talked earlier about the way performers get caught up in the demands of the business and how it affects their creative output. Does songwriting come less easily to you now? Do you feel yourself caught in a kind of rat race?

PRINCE: That happens more now, yeah. But as far as my songwriting is concerned, it's kind of going backwards. See, it's interesting—another reason I think I didn't get the "big deal" when I first came to New York, when I was younger, was because I was writing things that a cat with ten albums would have out, like seven-minute laments that were, y'know, gone. I wrote like I was rich, like I had been everywhere and seen everything and been with every woman in the world. But I liked that. I always liked fantasy and fiction—I used to write stories when I was younger. Like "Baby," from the first album—that was one of the songs that really blew Warner Bros. away 'cause it was about a cat getting a girl pregnant . . .

Now I like to just wait, to get in a different frame of mind, to get off the road. Because the only thing you can write on the road is about the concerts or about women. Other than that, you're in your hotel room, and all you can concern yourself with is the album you just did and how to make it best come across to people. When I'm off the road, then I lead my life.

SCHWARTZ: How about your stage show? Like don't you think you look a little silly to some people when you're up there in a jockstrap?

PRINCE: Maybe to people who only read about it, but I think the people who come to see it already expect it and wanna get into that [i.e., his underpants]. I've gotten a lot of criticism from outsiders, but once they see the show they understand why I wear what I wear. The show's real athletic and we run around a lot. and I have to be real comfortable. The decision was left up to me, and when I thought about what I was most comfortable in, it's what I sleep in . . . I just can't stand clothes.

SCHWARTZ: What comes first in the making of your records. Where do you start?

PRINCE: Hmmm . . . Strange as it may sound, this last album, a lot of it was done right there on the spot, writing and recording. That's how a lot of the stranger tunes came out . . . Most of the stuff was written on guitar—that's why the album is pretty guitar-oriented. I'd just got that real raggedy guitar and it sounded real cool to me. But like I said, I guess that's where the lines came from, the swearing and like that—it's basically what I was feeling at the time.

See, this album, it was all supposed to be demo tapes, that's what they started out to be. The previous albums were done in California, where they have better studios—I'd never wanted to do an album in Minneapolis. So they were demos, and I brought them out to the Coast and played them for the management and the record company. They said, "The sound of it is fine. The songs we ain't so sure about. We can't get this on the radio. It's not like your last album at all." And I'm going, "But it's like me. More so than the last album, much more so than the first one." We went back and forth, and they finally released it . . .

I don't know how anybody could spend a million dollars on an album. I couldn't take that long to make a record—if I did, it would be, like, a ten-album set. My album took about twelve days for the tracks, and about a week and a half for mixing. If you really listen to it, you'll hear that a lot of the harmonies aren't perfect, that I was just singing whatever I felt, playing whatever I felt. The rhythm tracks I kept pretty basic. I didn't try a lotta fancy stuff so I didn't have to go back and do things over.

SCHWARTZ: Where do you go from here?

PRINCE: Well, radio or no radio, we're just gonna keep playing until enough people hear us, that's all. I don't care if it sells so much as I want people to understand it, to give them the chance to see and hear it. Just from talking to kids on the street and people I meet—a lotta people didn't even know the songs, you could tell 'cause they weren't singing along, but we had their attention. They never turned away. That means more to me than them running out and buying. I just want them to listen, that's all.

PRINCE'S FIRST EVER INTERVIEW FOR TELEVISION

INTERVIEW WITH STEVE FARGNOLI
MTV
NOVEMBER 15, 1985

You are about to see Prince in his first interview for television. Now, he took a stab at being interviewed in print a few months ago, but this is the first time Prince has ever agreed to talk in front of cameras. The questions were provided by MTV's news department and the person you will hear asking them, at Prince's request, is his manager Steve Fargnoli. Now, Prince is not alone here; the interview was shot at the filming of his new video, "America," and the people that you're going to see with him are extras from the video. For the first time on television, this is Prince.*

STEVE FARGNOLI: The first and most obvious question is, why have you decided to drop your media guard and do interviews? And why were you so secretive prior to this?

PRINCE: Well, as you can see, I've made a lot of friends here, but I was homesick and I missed America. I guess I just wanted to talk to somebody.

FARGNOLI: A lot of observers have remarked on your apparent need for control, and only with your two most recent albums, you gave credit to your band for composing, arranging,

---

*   Editor's note: This interview has been lightly edited for clarity.

and performing. It seems to us, from what we know of your personal background, that the need for control arose from your childhood and early teen years, when you had a total lack of control over your life and were shuttled from home to home. Is this the case? If not, how does the need for control and/or your current, more open stance relate to your music?

PRINCE: I was horrible. To be perfectly honest, I was surrounded by my friends, but nevertheless, we had a difference of opinion in a lot of situations—musically speaking, that is. A lot had to do with me not being quite sure exactly which direction I wanted to go in. Later on toward the *Controversy* period, I got a better grip on that. That's when we started to see more and more people participating in recording activities. Boom.

FARGNOLI: Someone in Minneapolis recently told us that several months ago they were in a studio there when David Rifkin, your sound engineer, walked in. They asked him what he thought of the new Prince album, *Around the World in a Day*. He said, "It's great, but wait 'til you hear the new album." Apparently, he meant you're already working on a new LP, and that this one would be a strong return to your funk roots. Is this true? Can you elaborate? What will it be called? When will it be due out, and what's the music like?

PRINCE: Don't you like surprises? Guess not. Ah, it is true I record very fast. It goes even quicker now that the girls help me—the girls, meaning, Wendy and Lisa. I don't really think

I left my funk roots anywhere along the line. *Around the World in a Day* is a funky album. Live it's even funkier.

FARGNOLI: Why did you make the announcement that there'd be no singles or videos from that LP, and then start issuing singles and making videos anyway?

PRINCE: Because I wanted this album to be listened to, judged, and critiqued as a whole. It's hard to take a trip, go around the block, and stop when the trip is four hundred miles. Dig?

FARGNOLI: Speaking of singles and videos, your latest is "America." This is one of the most political songs you've ever done. Could you tell us what the song is supposed to say to people? For example, is it straightforwardly patriotic or more complicated than that?

PRINCE: Straightforwardly patriotic.

FARGNOLI: You directed the "America" video, and you also directed "Raspberry Beret." How do you approach directing a video? Do you consult others to keep a certain perspective when directing yourself?

PRINCE: Yes, definitely. When directing myself, I consult Steve [Fargnoli], my manager. On directing other Paisley Park artists, I consult the artists first and foremost. One of the things I try to do with the things I direct—namely for our acts—is go for the different, the out-of-the-norm, "the avant-purple," so to speak. And the thing that's unique about the situation I'm in now with these people is that they all know who they are, and they agree with me when we say the one thing we produce is the alternative. If someone wants to go along for that ride, then cool.

FARGNOLI: Tell us as much as you can about *Under The Cherry Moon*. What's the plot, what kind of characters, what kind of music, how many songs, what can we expect?

PRINCE: It's a French film. It's a black-and-white French film, and ah, she's in it [*points at Emmanuelle who is standing in the audience*] And her name's Emmanuelle Sallet, that's her name. [*Makes a face at Emmanuelle*] What?

EMMANUELLE SALLET: Where the hoes at?

PRINCE: What? Wait, Rome. Come here, man. [*Jerome Benton enters from off-screen*] This is Jerome Benton.

JEROME BENTON: Voilà. *Enchanté.* [*playfully shakes Prince's hand*]

PRINCE: He plays the landlord, we live together.

BENTON: [*mimicking a scene*] How much for the hat?

PRINCE: Three million, I got it in a divorce settlement.

BENTON: I'll settle for that.

PRINCE: Get out!

BENTON: Okay, cool, I'm raising the rent.

PRINCE: Emmanuelle can explain the film better. She can explain, to that camera, that one [*points at a camera offscreen, perspective shifts*], that pretty one.

SALLET: [*speaking in French; subtitles are provided*] It's a very beautiful black-and-white film, full of fantastic characters. It's a story of a pianist named Christopher and a very, very rich girl named Mary-Sharon. And they fall in love. In the film, I am a completely crazy girl with pigtails and miniskirts and I am the concierge, voilá.

PRINCE: Thank you. That was excellent.

SALLET: I will go get your Cadillac, okay?

PRINCE: Cadillac? [*laughs*] Oh no. [*looks directly at the camera*] I don't drive no Cadillac, all right? I used to. [*Emanuelle scoffs offscreen*] What? I don't anymore!

FARGNOLI: Speaking of movies, when and how did you first get the idea for *Purple Rain*? Did you really spend a year or so taking notes in a purple notebook, like some people have said?

PRINCE: Yes.

FARGNOLI: Did you ever think *Purple Rain*, the movie and the album, would be as big as they were?

PRINCE: I don't know.

FARGNOLI: Now that *Purple Rain* has made you such a huge superstar, do you worry about the possibility of a backlash against you?

PRINCE: One thing I'd like to say is that I don't live in a prison. I am not afraid of anything. I haven't built any walls around myself, and I am just like anyone else. I need love and water, and I'm not afraid of a backlash because, like I say, there are people who will support my habits as I have supported theirs. I don't really consider myself a superstar. I live in a small town, and I always will. I can walk around and be me. That's all I want to be, that's all I ever try to be. I didn't know what was going happen. I'm just trying to do my best and if somebody dug it then [*blows a kiss to the camera*].

FARGNOLI: A lot of people were offended by what they saw as sexism in *Purple Rain*.

PRINCE: Now, wait, wait. I didn't write *Purple Rain*. Someone else did. And it was a story, a fictional story, and should be perceived that way. Violence is something that happens in everyday life, and we were only telling a story. I wish it was looked at that way, because I don't think anything we did was unnecessary. Sometimes, for the sake of humor, we may've gone overboard. And if that was the case, then I'm sorry, but it was not the intention. Give a brother a break.

FARGNOLI: Speaking of brothers, some have criticized you for selling out to the white rock audience with *Purple Rain*, and leaving your black listeners behind. How do you respond to that?

PRINCE: Oh, come on, come on! Cufflinks like this cost money, okay? [*Holds up his cufflinks to the camera*] Let's be frank. Can we be frank? If we can't do nothing else, we might as well be frank. [*Blows kisses at the camera*] Seriously, I was brought up in a black-and-white world—black and white, night and day, rich and poor. I listened to all kinds of music when I was young, and when I was younger, I always said that one day I would play all kinds of music and not be judged for the color of my skin but the quality of my work, and hopefully that will continue. There are a lot of people out there that understand this, because they support me and my habits, and I support them and theirs.

FARGNOLI: You gave André Cymone the song "Dance Electric" for his new album. You two had some kind of falling out a few years back. When and how did you patch things up?

PRINCE: I saw André in a discotheque one night and grabbed him by his shirt and said, "Come on, I got this hit. You know I got this hit, don't you? 'Dance Electric?'" "Yeah," he said." "It's great." "You need it, you need it. No . . ." He started to walk away and I said," Hey, come here, don't you play, 'no, no, no.' You're not crazy, I'm crazy. I'm the one that's crazy, okay? So what're you going to do? You going to come by?" And he said, "For real? You ain't mad or nothing?" And I said, "No, so, what? Yeah. Tomorrow? Noon? Cool."

FARGNOLI: How do you feel about Jesse Johnson leaving the Time? Have you heard his album, and if so, what do you think of it?

PRINCE: Jesse and Morris and Jerome and Jimmy and Terry had the makings of one of the greatest R&B bands in history. I could be a little pretentious in saying that, but it's truly the way I feel. There's no one that could wreck a house like they could. I was a bit troubled by their demise, but like I said before, it's important that one's happy first and foremost. And, as far as Jesse's record goes, chocolate. You know?

FARGNOLI: There are rumors that the Revolution may record an album of its own.

PRINCE: I don't know. It'd be too strange. They're very talented people, but they're [*makes a spastic motion with his hands*], and together we're [*draws his hands parallel*]. I'd rather stay here [*parallel*], than [*spastic*].

FARGNOLI: Have you changed your mind about touring since you announced the *Purple Rain* tour would be your last?

PRINCE: No. I don't plan on touring for a while. There are so many other things to do.

FARGNOLI: It was obvious from the *Purple Rain* tour that, with the extended jams on some of these songs, you were paying tribute to James Brown. Would you agree? Who, besides

James Brown, were your major musical inspirations and influences? Hendrix? Clinton? Sly Stone?

PRINCE: James Brown played a big influence in my style. When I was about ten years old, my stepdad put me on stage with him, and I danced a little bit until the bodyguard took me off. The reason I liked James Brown so much is that, on my way out, I saw some of the finest dancing girls I ever seen in my life. And I think, in that respect, he influenced me by his control over his group. Another big influence was Joni Mitchell. She taught me a lot about color and sound, and to her, I'm very grateful.

FARGNOLI: Your father is a musician, too. Have you ever, or would you ever, try to get your father's music released on an album?

PRINCE: I did. He co-wrote "Computer Blue," "The Ladder," and several tunes on the new album. He's full of ideas. It'd be wonderful to put out an album on him, but he's a little bit crazier than I am.

FARGNOLI: You've said that you are surprised that people compare you to Hendrix.

PRINCE: A lot has to do with the color of my skin, and that's not where it's at. It really isn't. Hendrix is very good. Fact. There will never be another one like him, and it would be a pity to try. I strive for originality in my work, and hopefully, it'll be perceived that way.

FARGNOLI: Can you tell us about Paisley Park?

PRINCE: Paisley Park is an alternative. I'm not saying it's greater or better. It's just something else. It's multicolored, and it's very fun.

FARGNOLI: What are your religious beliefs?

PRINCE: I believe in God. There is only one God. And I believe in an afterworld. Hopefully we'll all see it. I have been accused of a lot of things contrary to this, and I just want people to know that I'm very sincere in my beliefs. I pray every night, and I don't ask for much. I just say, "thank you" all the time.

PLEASED TO MEET YOU . . .

INTERVIEW WITH ADRIAN DEEVOY
Q MAGAZINE
JULY 1994

. . . Hope you've guessed my name. For the first time since God alone knows when, the Artist talks exclusively and extensively about identity, insecurity, George Michael, Nelson Mandela, ballet, boogie, opera, orgasm, freedom, and the future. "I follow the advice of my spirit," he tells Adrian Deevoy.

HIS NAME IS NOT PRINCE. And he is not funky. His name is Albert. And he is lurching across the dance floor in search of accommodating company. Slightly balding and chunkier than he looks in photographs, he moors behind a gyrating female and clumsily interfaces.

Up on the stage another man whose name is not Prince says, "This is dedicated to Prince Albert, the funkiest man in Monaco." It's a wonder he can get the words out with his tongue buried so deep in his cheek. Prince Albert beams and grinds arhythmically on. The Artist laughs, throws a swift shape and stops the funk on the one. It's his party and he'll lie if he wants to.

One hundred and twenty people have been invited to the Stars 'N' Bars club in Monte Carlo for this most exclusive of celebrations. The champagne is free, the spirits are freer, and the house band is possibly the best live act on the planet. You probably remember them as Prince and the New Power

Generation. They're still the NPG but he's not Prince anymore. He is ⚥ (to give him his full title). Sir Hieroglyphicford for short.

Ursula Andress is at the bar, sipping sensually at a flute of champagne. A few generations and a couple of yards along, Claudia Schiffer is doing likewise. It's that sort of a do. Everyone is wearing impossibly shiny shoes and gold epaulets. If God weren't resting his suave old soul, you'd expect David Niven to walk in with Peter Wyngarde on his arm. Without trying too hard, you can imagine Fellini standing in the corner saying, "Christ, this is weird!" Quite what the gnarled jet-setters are making of the music program is anyone's guess. At 1:15 a.m. the Barry Manilow tape was exchanged for a stripped-down five-piece (and non-stop disco dancer Mayte—pronounced My Tie—Garcia) who have just embarked upon the most daunting funk experience of a lifetime. A knot of maybe fifteen perfumed debs cluster around the lip of the stage. Naturally you join them and find yourself standing so close to the Artist Formerly Known as Prince (AFKAP to use the diminutive) that you can hear him singing unamplified behind his microphone.

As the franc-trillionaires dance like your dad or simply stand looking bemused, a set of entirely new material is unleashed: a slamming funk madhouse named "Now"; a total headshag of a thing called "Interactive"; "Glam Slam Boogie," a swinging R&B shuffle; this scorching rap, "Days Of Wild"; "Space," a superb mid-paced chug; a Prince-of-yore smutathon which boasts the chorus "Pop goes the zipper"; "Race," another blistering rap and a freshly minted song which may not have been called "Jogging Machine."

Amazingly, despite performing for over two hours and dancing like an amphetamined primate, he doesn't break sweat. It's only during the very last song (during which he takes to calling out "Bass—hallowed be thy name" and "You know you're funky!") that minute moist tresses begin to glisten at the back of his neck. Shirtless now, you can't help but notice as he cavorts on the floor with Mayte that here is a man who has no truck with underwear. The trained medical eye can also detect, through sheer yellow matador trousers, that he is circumcised. And she isn't. It is indecently, maybe even illegally, sexy. "Doesn't anyone have to go to work tomorrow?" he asks rhetorically as the monied merry-makers bay for another encore. "Guess not."

THE ARTIST'S CAMP ARE AN ODD CREW: all are deeply aware of the idiosyncrasies of their bonsai boss—and they call him "Boss"—but they hold him in unutterably high esteem. One lunchtime, his American PR, face poker-straight, tells me that her charge is "an instrument of God." Over drinks, his European PR is a little more terrestrial: "He doesn't talk a lot," he says, reflecting on the Artist's visit, a few days ago, to his newly opened London shop. "He just came in and sat on the stairs sucking a lollipop. Then he wandered around for a while, looking at things. Of course, the next day I get long lists of changes he wants made."

The band plainly find his celebrity both a convenient distraction and a bit of a laugh. They are more than used to fencing questions about their commander, invariably dismissing enquiries with "He's just a regular cat like you and me," but in their hearts they know he isn't. I ask them one Fleet Street–type question about their shrift: "Is he Mayte's boyfriend?" "No," they say firmly. "She don't have a boyfriend."

Amusingly, among the entourage, the "P" word is rarely mentioned for fear it might result in the P45 word. There is a mild panic when a poster advertising his appearance at Monte Carlo's World Music Awards is spotted with the dread legend on it. In the blink of an eye the name is erased and the now familiar gold unisex symbol drawn in its place. "If he'd seen that," says a relieved minder, "he might have just turned around and gone home."

A telling scene occurs one night as the band are sitting around talking nonsense and drinking beer in the lobby of the oppressively posh Hotel De Paris. A huge horde of fans have gathered outside having heard that their hero is dining with Prince Albert tonight and will soon be emerging from the hotel. At 8:30, the Artist ghosts up by your side (you soon learn that he has this unnerving habit of just appearing) and in an unimaginably deep voice asks, "Shall I go out the front?" He is resplendent in full battle dress: a jacket made from what once must have been fold doily, lace strides, heels, walking cane, and lollipop. "Yeah," cry the band, "go out the front! Freak 'em out!" With the cheekiest of smirks, he pops the lolly decisively into his mouth and steps boldly out through the revolving door. The crowd screech his old name as, surrounded by three minders, he steps—head down, mouth corners curling knowingly—into a waiting car.

Only once during our five-day stay do we see the Artist out of his stage gear. He is in a lift heading down to have his hair re-teased and is wearing a black jumper, leather jeans, and impenetrable dark glasses, presumably because he hasn't bothered to put any makeup on. He looks remarkably pale but then he has just got up. It's 5:00 p.m.

Similarly, the only time you truly find him off-duty is when you wander early into the empty Stars 'N' Bars club and he is standing on the dance floor on his own, picking out a riff on a bass guitar. After thrumbing absently for a while he mutters "Sounds like shit" to himself. Then the enigmatic song and dance man looks over to the technicians and says, "Can we get separate EQ for the bass in the monitors?"

Such was the success of the gig at Prince Albert's party, a decision is made to play the same club the following evening. Sadly, the show isn't nearly half as good. It is merely transcendent.

"DO YOU FEEL READY TO MEET HIM?" It's been four days now. It's a little after midnight. You're not going to feel much readier. I'm escorted up to a small room that features a large white bed and not much else. The doors are open and, below, the guano-festooned roof of the Monte Carlo Casino looks monumentally unimpressive. The junior suite is the temporary home of the Artist's brother and head of security, Duane Nelson. In keeping with the name change game, he has been re-christened The Former Duane. The Artist's personal minder, a mightily be-blazered individual called Tracy, who looks and sounds alarmingly like Mike Tyson, informs us that "he" will be arriving soon.

Within a minute, there is a tiny commotion in the doorway and the Artist is suddenly standing before you like a virgin bride on her wedding night. Dressed completely in white silk and wearing full makeup, he only breaks a long floor-bound stare to flash one coquettish glance upward by way of a greeting. I'm introduced by name. He isn't. We are left alone.

An agreement made prior to this meeting stipulated, in no uncertain terms, that three rules were to be obeyed if intercourse of any description were to occur: firstly, that no tape recorder be used; secondly, that no notepad or pen be brought into the room; and thirdly, and most strangely, that no questions be asked. He wanted to enjoy a half-hour conversation unencumbered by the paraphernalia of nosy journalism.

He paces around the cramped boudoir in deliberate, even steps, as if he needed to fit the place with a new carpet and had forgotten his tape measure. He wanders out onto the balcony, still having not uttered a word and then comes back in, shutting the doors behind him. He is small but in perfect proportion, like a scale model of an adult. A doll, an Action Mannequin. He sits down next to me on the bed in a semi-lotus position and fixes his gaze on the middle distance, smiling secretly. No one has said anything for a full minute. Then he turns with this curious expression. It's somewhere between the shamed but surly look of someone that has been wrongly reprimanded and the suggestive yet intense glare of someone who is about to shag you. Oh no! He leans forward and you can smell him. It is just like the band said: he smells of flowers, music, and innocence. I smell of lager. Eventually, he says this:

"I don't say much."

Oh dear. Silence.

Why not?

He shrugs in slow-motion and looks sideways and downward. It's a sad, apologetic gesture, like he just killed your dog. This will serve as an answer for many of the questions he's initially asked. Once again. Why is that? Why don't you say much?

"You don't need to."

That doesn't bode well for this conversation really, does it?

"Guess not."

A different tack: "Speak to me only with thine eyes." Have you heard that phrase?

"Mm."

He turns on the bed and laughs, rolling his eyes to heaven. He is wearing an extraordinary amount of slap—foundation, eyeliner, black mascara (on lashes of which Bambi is alleged to be fiercely jealous), brown eye shadow on the outermost corners of his lids. He has the most slender line of facial hair that runs from one temple, down his cheek across his upper lip and up the other side. There are black, phallic rockets on the sleeves of his shirt.

We look at each other for a while. It isn't quite uncomfortable, more exhilarating, like a first date. In keeping with this, I say: "You look lovely, by the way."

He exhales almost sexually, bites his lower lip and whispers, "Why, thank you."

This is becoming ludicrous. We've got thirty minutes, and ten of those have just been swallowed up with nothing more than a handful of sighs, some peculiar body language, and one dodgy chat-up line to show for it. I decide to forget the rules and fire a volley of questions at him.

How did you feel when you heard Jimi Hendrix for the first time? He stops and thinks and arranges his hands in a steeple in front of his mouth.

"That was before Puerto Rico," he says quietly and, to be honest, mystifyingly. "I can't remember much before then. That was before I changed my name."

Why have you changed your name?

"I acted on the advice of my spirit."

Do you normally do that. Is it reliable, your spirit's advice? "Of course."

Is it significant that you've changed your name?

"It's very significant."

Did you dream last night?

He frowns. "No, can't remember. Although I had a dream recently and I was telling Mo Ostin (Chairman of Warner Bros. Records) to be all a man and not half a man."

Last night I dreamt I saw this article in print. Believe it or not, the headline was Funny Little Fucker.

Seriously.

He laughs. "Oh."

Do you fall in love easily?

"No."

You're a slow burner then?

"Uh-huh."

It isn't going tremendously well. Knocking it on the head and suggesting we just go out for a curry begins to seem like an excellent idea. Then something highly bizarre and Prince-like happens: a sound starts to crackle through a previously unnoticed and inert TV. Without missing a beat, he nods toward the set and says, "It's a sign. It's a sign that we should go to my room." He makes for the door, leading with his shoulders. Duane appears in the hall and asks what the problem is. "A sound came through the TV," explains the Artist. "It's a sign." "Nah," says Duane, "you probably just sat on the remote control." And with that, he ushers us back into the bedroom to continue our "conversation."

ADRIAN DEEVOY: Do you think you're underrated as a lyricist?

THE ARTIST: Well, underrated by who? Against what? You know? Some people get them. That's what counts.

DEEVOY: Do people not get the humor in your work?

THE ARTIST: Maybe, but there's a lot of things that I don't get the humor in.

DEEVOY: What's the most moving piece of music you've heard recently?

THE ARTIST: [*Long, sigh-strewn pause*] Sonny's bass solo last night.

DEEVOY: What is your preoccupation with sex all about? It features in nearly all your songs. Does sex really loom that large in your life?

THE ARTIST: My songs aren't all about sex. People read that into them.

DEEVOY: But sex is such a dominant theme. Your new song called "Come" is unarguably about orgasm.

THE ARTIST: Is it? That's your interpretation? Come where? Come to whom? Come for what?

DEEVOY: Oh, come on!

THE ARTIST: [*Laughs*] That's just the way you see it. It's in your mind.

This is the first subject he warms to: different perceptions. How one man's meat is another man's muesli. This, he explains, is why we can't label music, feelings, people. He says something convoluted like: everything is something else to everyone. When I begin to ask him about how he thinks other people perceive him, it obviously touches a nerve. He adopts the voice of an especially demented mynah bird and asks, "Are you normal? Are you normal? Is that what you're asking me? Do I think I'm normal? Yes, I do. I think I'm normal. I am normal."

DEEVOY: What happens in your life when you're not doing music?

THE ARTIST: [*Hikes, eyebrows, looks incredulous*] When I'm not doing music?

DEEVOY: Do you have a life outside of your work?

THE ARTIST: Yes.

DEEVOY: And what does that involve?

THE ARTIST: [*Pinteresque pause*] Have you never read about me? I'm a very private person.

DEEVOY: I'm not prying, I'm just interested.

THE ARTIST: I know. I understand.

The subject of his recording contract with Warner Bros. comes up, as does the topic of Prince's work—he speaks about Prince in the third person. Whether or not Prince the recording artist is finished, consigned to the bunker of history, is unclear. He says several times that the body of work is complete but later admits that he hasn't ruled out the possibility of adding to it, under the name Prince or otherwise, in the future.

DEEVOY: Is it possible to shed an entire personality?

THE ARTIST: It's not like it's a real personality.

DEEVOY: It's a person then?

THE ARTIST: Yeah, I think it is.

DEEVOY: Have you turned your back on pop music?

THE ARTIST: What's pop music? It's different things to different people.

DEEVOY: Beatles-derived four-chord tunes that everyone can sing along to.

THE ARTIST: Still don't help. Is "The Most Beautiful Girl" pop music? I can't say? You can't say.

He mentions George Michael's court case for the first time. It's a subject he'll return to with astonishing regularity and persistence. At one point, he almost shouts, "Why can't George Michael do what he wants? Why can't he write a ballet if he wants to?" What he is talking about is artistic freedom and its place in the future. By the end of the rant, and it is a rant, I suggest that he should get in touch with George Michael as he might find such supportive words encouraging. "Oh," he says breezily. "We speak."

DEEVOY: What do you think about when you're playing a guitar solo?

THE ARTIST: I'm normally just listening.

DEEVOY: You look like you're about to cry sometimes.

THE ARTIST: Really? Mm. Maybe.

DEEVOY: You seem at your most relaxed on stage.

THE ARTIST: If it's all going well, I'm pretty happy up there. It's a very natural thing for me.

DEEVOY: Offstage you seem to be having a good old laugh at us sometimes.

He laughs.

The categorization of music is another area which gets his goat. How on earth can we categorize something like music when everybody hears and feels it differently? How many people do you know that have just one type of music in their record collections? None, right? You don't get home and think, I'll listen to some ambient jazz punk, do you? You just have a mood in your head and yet we, or at least the record companies, feel the need to compartmentalize everything. Tell you what, when you play a song live, and it's a jam, man, and you think up some little vocal line and everyone is still singing that when you've left that stage—that's marketing. Period. Wouldn't it be great if someone made an album and gave it away for free? Like air. You could just have it. Anyway, what type of music do The Sundays play? Is it pop, indie, rock? Who cares?

When eventually, I say that anyone who heard Prince play would assume that his new direction was big funk, he says cryptically, "You could ask those people what they saw and they might say that they didn't see Prince play at all . . ."

DEEVOY: Do you ever have a problem translating the sounds you hear in your head into music?

THE ARTIST: No, that's never been a problem. The problem is getting it all out before another idea comes along.

DEEVOY: Do you exhaust people?

THE ARTIST: [*Laughs*] Yes, I do.

DEEVOY: A joke: you used to be called Prince and then you were Victor. Why not just call yourself Vince?

THE ARTIST: I read that somewhere. I was never called Victor. That was the line in the song, "I will be called Victor," I never called myself Victor.

He launches into a stream of consciousness monologue about names. What they mean. This seems to confuse him. He has, he says, a friend called Gilbert Davidson, and one day he said to Gilbert, Who is David? Is he your father? No, said Gilbert. Is he your grandfather? No. Then, man, you'd better look back and find out who he is. Then Prince started thinking, My name is Nelson. Who was Nel? My mother? No. My grandmother? Uh-uh. Then he thought, Maybe she's someone that I don't want to know about.

DEEVOY: I asked the band, individually, what you smell of?

THE ARTIST: What I smell of? What'd Sonny say?

DEEVOY: He said you smell of music.

THE ARTIST: [*Delighted smile*] That's a good answer, Sonny. That's a like, yeah, yeah, let's have the next question type answer, isn't it?

DEEVOY: And I asked them to sum you up in one word. The word one of them chose was, Wow!

THE ARTIST: [*Laughs*] Who said that? No, let me guess. Was it Michael?

DEEVOY: Yes.

THE ARTIST: That's funny. Wow. We don't normally talk about that kind of stuff.

Now he's getting excited. He has moved to a chair and is sitting with his boots—high-heeled, silver stage numbers covered in mini mirrors—up on the counterpane. At one pint, while agreeing about something with particular enthusiasm, I grab hold of his boot. He doesn't flinch, but his toes wriggle inside. He has left behind the cautious customer of yesterhour and is freewheeling through the thoughts as they enter his head. Suddenly it strikes you. Blimey! It's just like having a chat with a normal bloke.

DEEVOY: Tell me about the opera you've written.

THE ARTIST: I don't want to give too much away. It's just a story.

DEEVOY: What sort of story? A love story?

THE ARTIST: Could be.

DEEVOY: Did you write the libretto?

THE ARTIST: Yeah, [*he laughs at the pretentiousness of the word*] I wrote the story.

DEEVOY: Did you find opera difficult to get into?

THE ARTIST: I don't really listen to opera.

He had spoken to Placido Domingo earlier in the evening. "He said some very beautiful things, and you could sense that he had a feeling of all the power that was in the room and what it could achieve if we did something with it." While they were talking, the Artist got this tune in his head that he's going to get down pretty quickly.

DEEVOY: I've been told that you're an instrument of God.

THE ARTIST: Oh yeah, stuff's been written about that. Who said that?

DEEVOY: Your PR.

THE ARTIST: [*Laughs*] Really?

DEEVOY: Do you seriously feel like you are a conduit for some higher power?

THE ARTIST: No, I just practice a lot.

DEEVOY: Do you ever feel a certain telepathy exists between you and the NPG?

THE ARTIST: Sure, musically, that happens sometimes. But we rehearse too.

He tells a long story about the making of the video for "The Most Beautiful Girl in The World." They placed ads and got shedloads of letters and home videos back. They selected a cross-section of women all from different backgrounds and invited them to meet the Artist. He asked them what their dreams were and then to the best of his mortal abilities set about making those dreams come true. Like Jim'll fix it with O levels. Then they filmed the women watching footage of their fantasies. One of the women, and he gets quite emotional as he relates this, wrote to him afterward saying that although she was overweight, he had made her feel beautiful and she would lose weight with the intention of modeling one day.

DEEVOY: Is physical beauty an overrated virtue?

THE ARTIST: Yes. See, you understand.

DEEVOY: Did you sit on "The Most Beautiful Girl in The World" so Warner Bros. couldn't have it and you could release it on your own terms?

THE ARTIST: No, I didn't sit on it. I heard that I did that but I only wrote it recently.

DEEVOY: What would you have done if it had stiffed?

THE ARTIST: If it had stiffed? [*Laughs*] It wouldn't have mattered. I put the record out, that was the important thing. People got to hear it.

DEEVOY: Did you feel vindicated when it was so successful?

THE ARTIST: Well, it's nice when people appreciate what you do.

We discuss the future again. He says, "That's why I wanted you to help me—and I need some help with this—because you think that anything is possible." He peels off at a tangent. "In the future," he announces, "I might be interactive. You might be able to access me and tell me what to play." It's certainly a thought. He says he's found a new drummer "who plays things you can't even think. And if he wants to do an album of drum solos, then I'm prepared to go out on tour to finance that." He reveals that he's got a blues album completed and in the can and lets out a vocal wail of anguished guitar to illustrate just how good it is. He brings up Nelson Mandela and the current situation in South Africa. Mr. Mandela, as he calls him, must have had a very clear vision of what would happen. He envies this and would like to have that gift. Something of a basketball fan, he alludes to Magic Johnson time and time again. "He wants to form his own team," he says. "How long will that take?" He looks at his non-existing watch and shoots a look to the ceiling. "Look at South Africa," he says, palms upturned. "Bosnia. You can't tell people what to do for that long." He appears to be equating racial and artistic freedom, then he has to be prepared to put up with that Mick Hucknall jazz harmonica album, which, under these terms, could easily emerge. "But would that be a bad thing?" he asks, his argument crumbling. "OK," he concedes, giggling, "I guess you wouldn't have to listen to everything."

DEEVOY: Won't people say, "It's all very well Prince banging on about artistic freedom when we've got bills to pay and mundane reality to cope with." Aren't you speaking from a privileged position?

THE ARTIST: If you're shackled and restricted, it doesn't matter how much money you got. Money don't help. And I've got bills to pay. People at Paisley [Park], they're like my family, I have responsibility toward them.

DEEVOY: Would you like to have children?

THE ARTIST: That's something I haven't thought about.

DEEVOY: You've been thinking about the future so much and you haven't considered children?

THE ARTIST: No, but I'd like to contribute to the future generation.

HE'S TEARING UP AND DOWN THE ROOM now, having talked for almost an hour and a half. His voice has become excited and slipped up a key. Not quite KISS standards but getting there. Now and then, he slips into black slang.

He even belches once, very gently, but it's a belch nonetheless. It's like the Queen farting and lighting it. He enthuses about his new songs, "Now" and "Days of Wild." "What the fuck is that all about?" he asks, shimmying around the bed with one arm stiff behind his back, rapping the opening lines, which involve copious use of the oedipal compound noun. He raves about the genius of George Clinton, froths about his *Smell My Finger* album and is plainly in awe of his talents. "George is the funk," he explains breathlessly. He speaks about purity in music. "Rock 'n' roll, man," he says, "was so much better when people were hungry. It was better when you didn't automatically make money. When James [Brown] was putting out an album every four months, that was the stuff."

It's getting on for 2:00 a.m. now, and we have one final bash at distilling what he really wants to convey. Before that, he asks about magazine editorial practice and is stimulated by the fact that an article can go from writer to reader virtually untampered with. He speculates about producing music that you would listen to as you read this article. "That would be great, wouldn't it? And although I am an artist without a contract, that's just the sort of thing I can't do."

He recaps one last time: artistic freedom for everyone with fearlessness and limitlessness well of the fore; love and care to be liberally distributed and accepted; peace to reign; dolphins to leap; choirs of children to sing and, um, George Michael to write that ballet.

"So," he says spinning on his spangly heels. "Are we gonna party?" He dances toward the door, flicks a final seductive glance over his shoulder, and sashays out. Funny little fucker.

A PRINCE OF A GUY

INTERVIEW WITH CATHERINE CENSOR SHEMO
VEGETARIAN TIMES
OCTOBER 1997

MOST KNOW HIM as the guy with the symbol for a name—the rocker whose raunchy lyrics were quoted in Congress during the debate over parental advisories on recordings; the guy whose sense of style includes peek-a-boo clothing and bold gestures such as scrawling "slave" on his cheek during his disputes with Warner Bros. But there's a surprising side to The Artist Formerly Known as Prince.

The man behind the symbol is witty, political, compassionate, deeply spiritual—and vegetarian. He's also newly talkative. For much of his career, the Artist (as he is referred to by friends and even Mayte, his wife) rarely granted interviews. His reluctance to discuss the name change or other, more tragic aspects of his life (he and Mayte reportedly had a physically impaired son who died soon after birth), fueled rampant tabloid rumor.

But now, at thirty-eight, the Artist seems to have found his voice. And perhaps the reason is that he has a great deal to talk about: He finally owns the master tapes to his own work and his latest triple CD, *Emancipation*, has gone double platinum. He is deeply in love with his wife. Twenty-three-year-old Mayte ("my-TAY"), a dancer and former member of the Artist's band, the New Power Generation; together they have founded a charity, Love 4 One Another, that helps underprivileged kids and adults. And his vegetarianism—indeed much of his outlook on Life—has been inspired by his love for her.

If the Artist is still learning his way around a vegetarian refrigerator (Mayte describes his food preferences as "still kind of bland—he isn't used to the ethnic food that vegetarians eat"), he's both knowledgeable and outspoken about animal rights and human nutrition. In fact , the theme of animal rights has cropped up in the lyrics of two recent songs. One of them, "Joint 2 Joint," on the *Emancipation* CD, reveals a distinct preference for soy milk over dairy ("Oh great/Now you think you're my soul mate/You don't even know what kind of cereal I like/Wrong/Captain Crunch/With soymilk/Cuz cows are for calves"). The other, "Animal Kingdom," from his as yet unreleased CD *Truth*, takes an unnamed friend to task for singing the praises of cow's milk. That "friend" is apparently Spike Lee, who has appeared in the dairy industry's "milk mustache" ad campaign.

In an exclusive interview. we asked the Artist about everything from karma to Captain Crunch. Here's what he had to say:

CATHERINE CENSOR SHEMO: How, when, and why did you and Mayte become vegetarians?

THE ARTIST: I've not eaten red meat for about ten years now. Mayte for a lot longer. I've always had a preference for all things vegetarian but not until recently did I find out how good they were for you (in a physical sense).

CENSOR: How far have you taken your vegetarianism? The

lyrics on *Emancipation*'s "Joint 2 Joint" suggest you like soy milk on your cereal. Have you given up dairy and eggs as well as flesh foods?

THE ARTIST: We don't eat anything with parents. Complete vegans—both of us! The opening lyrics to "Animal Kingdom" [on the forthcoming *Truth* album] refer to a conversation between Spike and me about the benefits of cow's milk over human. I believe they are few.

CENSOR: Many people become vegetarian out of concern for their health, but I know that's not what motivated you and Mayte. Can you tell us how your beliefs affected this decision?

THE ARTIST: Thou shalt not kill means just that! We don't have to kill things to survive. In fact, the complete opposite happens: If you kill, you will die.

CENSOR: That sounds pretty dire. Speaking of dire: Some people think vegetarianism is all about denying yourself pleasure. Have you found this to be true? You don't strike me as the kind of guy who thinks sensual pleasure is negative.

THE ARTIST: Mayte and I get no pleasure from playing Russian roulette with food. Eating anything ridden with bacteria raises your chances for disease. Being sick is not pleasurable.

CENSOR: I gather that Mayte is the driving force behind your interest in vegetarianism. Would you have gotten there without her influence?

THE ARTIST: Mayte showed me how many different vegetarian dishes one could have and never miss the things you would imagine. I never was a big milk drinker anyway, but I really like vanilla soy milk. Being without my wife's influence is not a reality to me, so I don't speculate on life without her.

CENSOR: What changes have the two of you noticed since becoming vegetarians?

THE ARTIST: I actually enjoy eating more. I have more energy and most of all, my aura is stronger. One can actually feel one's karmic debt decrease with every meal. Mayte enjoys preparing meals for the two of us. It strengthens our bond.

CENSOR: Your practical, as well as philosophical, experience is of interest to us. Now that you're eating vegetarian meals, are you learning to cook differently? Do you have a chef who cooks for you? Do you have a favorite style of cuisine or a favorite meal?

THE ARTIST: Mayte cooks for us. She's always trying new things. The wonderful thing about vegetarianism is there is no favorite dish because there is no addiction. Non-vegetarians always speak about their favorite because it usually involves something artificial or something that doesn't belong in them. Ah, the universe keeps expanding!

CENSOR: I noticed that a major theme in your recent music is freedom. It's on tracks like "Animal Kingdom" and "Joint 2 Joint." Is this a new area of exploration for you, or has your freedom always been a central theme of even your early work? Has vegetarianism expanded the horizon of this concept?

THE ARTIST: Freedom has always been a theme in my work. Vegetarianism is a natural step for *anyone* seeking oneness with the spirit. The conscience is powerful (in a good way) when clear and weak when not.

CENSOR: Life can be pretty brutal. There's a lot of senseless pain and suffering in the world, and some people say "Why waste your time worrying about animals when so many people are suffering?" Are vegetarians wasting their compassion? Distracting themselves from human pain?

THE ARTIST: Compassion is an action word with no boundaries. It is never wasted. To eat a tomato and then replant it for your nutrition as opposed to killing a cow or a pig for your meal is reducing the amount of suffering in the world. Besides, pigs are too cute to die.

CENSOR: Do you worry that fans of your music might be put off by the message of songs like "Animal Kingdom" or by the public declaration of your vegetarianism?

THE ARTIST: Fan is short for "fanatic." I call my supporters "friends." My friends are very forward-thinking individuals. I'm not sure how many are meat eaters but soon all will know the consequences of a barbarian lifestyle. It's called karma! My music is dictated by the spirit. Not worrying about people's reaction is what has sustained me. I believe.

CENSOR: Speaking of worrying about the public: There are lots of people who think vegetarianism is weird. You're already the subject of lots of public speculation and gossip. Will declaring yourself vegetarian add fuel to that fire?

THE ARTIST: We'd rather be looked over than overlooked. In all seriousness, it's obvious that the world has problems, but doing nothing about it is foolish. We have holidays for dead presidents who stood for everything but freedom of the soul. We need an Animal Rights day when all the slaughterhouses shut down, and people don't eat anything they can't replace. Yeah!

CENSOR: Much has been made of your name change. Does that signify a reinvention of self? A rebirth? What has fallen away with the old name?

THE ARTIST: My name change is a complex issue not really suited for this discussion but what I can say is that it is much easier to separate the ego from the personality now. And I'm much happier since my name change.

CENSOR: Tell us about the new album and your latest projects. What can we look forward to next?

THE ARTIST: *Emancipation* [the current album] is a tour de force and what's best is that I finally own the master tape—so if you have any of my work and you like it, please support this project because it's the closest to my soul. Thank you for a chance to speak to the enlightened vegans of your magazine. We like being one of you!

SITES O' THE TIMES

INTERVIEW WITH BEN GREENMAN
YAHOO! INTERNET LIFE
OCTOBER 1997

In his early days, Prince was dismissed as a sensualist. Later on, when he started writing scriptural pop like *Lovesexy* and changed his name to an unpronounceable symbol, he was ridiculed as a spiritualist. All along the way, the Minneapolis multi-instrumentalist has been at once an avid consumer and a sharp critic of technology. The title song of *1999* fretted about nuclear weaponry, while the title song of *Sign O' the Times* mused on the folly of space travel in the wake of the *Challenger* disaster.

In recent years, the Artist has turned his attention toward interactive technologies, particularly the internet. Last year's triple album, *Emancipation*, included two songs about cyberspace—"Emale" and "My Computer," the latter of which sampled America Online's "Welcome," "You've got mail," and "Good-bye" sounds. The Love 4 One Another website launched this summer. And on the eve of his Jam of the Year tour, in mid-July, the Artist even drew more than 300,000 participants on an AOL chat. Because of his interest in the online medium, the Artist agreed to talk to *Yahoo! Internet Life* about his music, his fans, the future of the internet, and even cybersex.

BEN GREENMAN: When did you first go online?

THE ARTIST: I first went online alone 7 months ago, 2 the best of my recollection.

GREENMAN: How often do you go online?

THE ARTIST: When I am not on the road, maybe 3 or 4 times a week.

GREENMAN: Are there any sites that you think are especially good?

THE ARTIST: Love 4 One Another. I also like the news section on AOL.

GREENMAN: Are there any sites that you think are especially bad?

THE ARTIST: Bad is not a word I use unless I am describing a fine girl.

GREENMAN: Do you visit the alt.music.prince newsgroup? If so, what do you think about it?

THE ARTIST: I have seen it once or twice. It seems 2 just be a place 4 trading bootlegs.

GREENMAN: Do you visit the fan websites devoted to your music? If so, what do you think about them?

THE ARTIST: There are many I really dig. I'm really interested in getting all my friends 2gether on one site.

GREENMAN: How do you feel about tape-trading and bootleg CDs? Have you ever bought a bootleg of one of your own performances?

THE ARTIST: I understand their existence. But I don't agree with buying and selling stolen property. Trading isn't so despicable.

GREENMAN: What about all the rumors, speculation, and criticism about you that circulates online? Is it amusing or annoying? For example, someone wrote to the newsgroup to complain that you always release the weakest songs from albums as singles.

THE ARTIST: Opinion is how the world changes. That's cool, but lies and rumors don't deserve response. Also consider that any release of a single is only an advertisement 4 the album. And guess which 1 costs more?

GREENMAN: On your newsgroup, some people have worried that the charity aspect of the Love 4 One Another site will be overwhelmed by the fandom aspect. Are you concerned about this?

THE ARTIST: Not in the least bit. Negative souls are bored by things like charity. They obviously think the world revolves because of something other than love.

GREENMAN: Why did you close your previous official site, The Dawn?

THE ARTIST: Because without my involvement, the message was getting blurred. In my humble opinion, the dawn occurs when spiritual enlightenment takes place. When 1 learns of his or her relationship 2 everything on Earth and the universe. The new website will mirror the positive aspects of the dawn. In my rush 2 enlighten myself and others, I tried 2 "buffalo the vibe thru" when it was not ready. Love 4 One Another is the dawn.

GREENMAN: Since you broke with Warner Bros., you've explored alternatives to traditional distribution. Do you have any plans to sell your music directly to consumers via the Net?

THE ARTIST: Yes. NPG Records will sell as well as give away a lot of new and old music over the internet in the not-too-distant future.

GREENMAN: Will record labels eventually disappear?

THE ARTIST: The writing is on the wall. Other souls were successful in their divide-and-conquer approach 4 a while. But now that we communicate with each other on a worldwide basis, the need 4 an "in4mation censor" is no longer a reality. The process of manufacturing and delivering music 2 a "friend" is not brain surgery.

GREENMAN: On *Emancipation*, you wrote two songs about

the internet —"Emale" and "My Computer." What was the inspiration for those songs?

THE ARTIST: A man who unsuccessfully tried 2 "play me" was the catalyst 4 "Emale." I imagined his woman looking at her computer and being seduced by her "emale." "My Computer" was inspired by some of the insightful talks I have had with many positive people on the Net.

GREENMAN: "Emale" is about cybersex. What do you think about cybersex? Have you ever done it?

THE ARTIST: Ain't nothin' like the real thang.

GREENMAN: In *Graffiti Bridge*, you use a Macintosh. Do you still use a Mac?

THE ARTIST: My art department does. My wife owns an IBM. That's what I use.

GREENMAN: Does "Computer Blue" have anything at all to do with computers?

THE ARTIST: It may. That hasn't revealed itself yet.

GREENMAN: What is the place of computer technology in composing new music?

THE ARTIST: I try 2 let the song dictate its own direction. If one makes music with a computer, one has 2 be satisfied with the computer's limitations (and there are many, especially when it comes 2 music), though some songs only "sing" when programmed on a computer.

GREENMAN: On the *Interactive* enhanced CD and *The Gold Experience* LP, there's a lot of talk about interactivity—"over 500 experiences to choose from," etc. Have you ever thought about creating new types of music especially for the internet-interactive environments, personalized songs, and so on?

THE ARTIST: Yes. We are in discussion now 2 design a computer that can be a member of my band as well as interact with the audience. I have always been intrigued by the notion of being inside a computer.

GREENMAN: OK, now for some final questions. If you were to write a theme song for the internet, what would it be called, and what would it sound like?

THE ARTIST: "New World."

GREENMAN: The Net seems to attract lots of studio-obsessed musicians. Is surfing the Net at all like being in the studio?

THE ARTIST: No, no, no, no, no, no, no, no!

GREENMAN: Do you think "Shockadelica" is your best song? If not, why not?

THE ARTIST: "Shockadelica" is about a witch. "The Holy River" is about redemption. I am no judge.

GREENMAN: What do you think about the Warner Bros. site?

THE ARTIST: I never visit their site.

GREENMAN: Most of the online search engines still have you listed as "Prince," rather than the androgyny symbol, "The Artist Formerly Known as Prince," or "The Artist." How do you feel about that?

THE ARTIST: 2 each his own. I am a progressor. Some like the past. I don't mind.

GREENMAN: This may sound nuts, but does the Camille alter ego, which you used on *Sign O' the Times*, have anything to do with the famous nineteenth-century hermaphrodite Herculine Barbin, who was nicknamed Camille? If so, my younger brother will be very, very happy, since he has spent roughly a decade trying to convince me of this.

THE ARTIST: Your brother is very wise.

GREENMAN: And finally, will you be online in 1999?

THE ARTIST: In some form, yes.

SOUP WITH PRINCE

INTERVIEW WITH CLAIRE HOFFMAN
NEW YORKER
NOVEMBER 2008

The 30,000-square-foot Italianate villa, built this century by Vanna White's ex-husband, looks like many of the other houses in Beverly Park, a gated community in L.A., except for the bright-purple carpet that spills down the front steps to announce its new tenant: Prince. One afternoon just before the election, Prince invited a visitor over. Inside, the place was done up in a generic Mediterranean style, although there were personal flourishes here and there—a Lucite grand piano with a gold-colored "Artist Formerly Known as Prince" symbol suspended over it, purple paisley pillows on a couch. Candles scented the air, and New Age music played in the living room, where a TV screen showed images of bearded men playing flutes. Prince padded into the kitchen, a small fifty-year-old man in yoga pants and a big sweater, wearing platform flip-flops over white socks, like a geisha.

"Would you like something to eat?" he asked, sidling up to the counter. Prince's voice was surprisingly deep, like that of a much larger man. He picked up a copy of *21 Nights*, a glossy volume of photographs that he had just released. It is his first published book, a collection of highly stylized photographs of him taken during a series of gigs in London last year. "I'm really proud of this," he said. Short original poems and a CD accompany the photographs. (Sample verse: "Who eye really am only time will tell/ 2 the almighty life 4ce that

grows stronger with every chorus/ Yes give praise, lest ye b
among . . . the guilty ones.")

Limping slightly, Prince set off on a walk around his new
bachelor pad. Glass doors opened onto acres of backyard, and
a hot tub bubbled in the sunlight. "I have a lot of parties," he
explained. In the living room, he'd installed purple thrones
on either side of a fireplace, and, nearby, along a hallway, he
had hung photographs of himself, in a Moroccan villa, in
various states of undress. At the end of the hall, a gauzy cur-
tain fluttered in a doorway. "My room," he said. "It's private."

Prince has lived in Los Angeles since last spring, after
spending years in Minneapolis, holding court in a complex
called Paisley Park, where he made thousands of songs, far
away from the big labels. Seven years ago, he became a Jehovah's Witness. He said that he had moved to L.A. so that he
could understand the hearts and minds of the music moguls.
"I wanted to be around people, connected to people, for work,"
he said. "You know, it's all about religion. That's what unites
people here. They all have the same religion, so I wanted to sit
down with them, to understand the way they see things, how
they read Scripture."

Prince had his change of faith, he said, after a two-year-
long debate with a musician friend, Larry Graham. "I don't
see it really as a conversion," he said. "More, you know, it's a
realization. It's like Morpheus and Neo in *The Matrix*." He at-
tends meetings at a local Kingdom Hall, and, like his fellow-
witnesses, he leaves his gated community from time to time
to knock on doors and proselytize. "Sometimes people act
surprised, but mostly they're really cool about it," he said.

Recently, Prince hosted an executive who works for

Philip Anschutz, the Christian businessman whose company owns the Staples Center. "We started talking red and blue," Prince said. "People with money—money like that—are not affected by the stock market, and they're not freaking out over anything. They're just watching. So here's how it is: you've got the Republicans, and basically they want to live according to this." He pointed to a Bible. "But there's the problem of interpretation, and you've got some churches, some people, basically doing things and saying it comes from here, but it doesn't. And then on the opposite end of the spectrum you've got blue, you've got the Democrats, and they're, like, 'You can do whatever you want.' Gay marriage, whatever. But neither of them is right."

When asked about his perspective on social issues—gay marriage, abortion—Prince tapped his Bible and said, "God came to earth and saw people sticking it wherever and doing it with whatever, and he just cleared it all out. He was, like, 'Enough.'"

Later, in the dining room, eating a bowl of carrot soup, he talked about an encounter that he described as a "teaching moment." "There was this woman. She used to come to Paisley Park and just sit outside on the swings," he said. "So I went out there one day and I was, like, 'Hey, all my friends in there say you're a stalker. And that I should call the police. But I don't want to do that, so why don't you tell me what you want to happen. Why are you here? How do you want this to end?' And she didn't really have an answer for that. In the end, all she wanted was to be seen, for me to look at her. And she left and didn't come back."

A FINAL VISIT WITH PRINCE: ROLLING STONE'S LOST COVER STORY

INTERVIEW WITH BRIAN HIATT
ROLLING STONE
JANUARY 2014

It is, in theory, a mundane sight, nothing 2 get excited about: just a fifty-five-year-old man in his suburban Minneapolis workplace, scrolling through a Windows Media Player library on a clunky Dell computer. An equally ordinary multi-line phone sits beside it, near a lit candle, bottled water, and some expensive-looking lotion. A huge old Xerox machine looms over the desk; a window at the far end of the room looks out onto barren trees and an empty, snow-lined highway. It's early evening on Saturday, January 25th, 2014, in Chanhassen, Minnesota.

The office is on the second floor of the 65,000-square-foot Paisley Park compound. The little guy sitting at the keyboard owns it all, had it all built back in the eighties. And Prince being Prince, it's fascinating to watch him do just about anything. The more ordinary the activity—clicking a mouse, say—the weirder it feels. Prince has a large Afro, and he's dressed in dark, diaphanous layers, with a vest over a flowing long-sleeved shirt, form-fitting grayish-black slacks, and sneakers with high Lucite heels that light up with every step. He's wearing obvious makeup—foundation, eyeliner, probably more. His thin, precision-trimmed mustache extends just past his lips in a semicircle.

On characteristically short notice, Prince invited me here to report what we intend to be his seventh *Rolling Stone* cover story. I spend seven hours at Paisley Park, and he sits for two lengthy, thoughtful, amiable interviews. I was told not to curse or to ask about the past; though I eventually violate both rules, he invites me to join him on the road later. In the end, however, he won't sit for a photo shoot, instead offering us pre-prepared, heavily retouched pictures. The whole thing falls through. I hold onto my reporting, assuming, all too correctly, that we will save the material for our next Prince cover.

That night, Prince doesn't look his age—doesn't look any particular age, really. He's very thin, but not fragile—a strict vegan who, by his own account, sometimes doesn't eat at all ("I have gone long periods with no food, and also water—people have to remind me to drink water because I always forget to do that"). He doesn't sleep enough, either, and he avoids sex: One of the most deliriously sensual performers who ever lived—the one who sang "Jack U Off" and "Gett Off" and "Do Me, Baby"—insists he's celibate. His reasons are both religious and "energy"-related ("The hunger turns into something else," he says), though he maintains close relationships with several young female singer-songwriters. He is, at this stage in his life, a kind of cheerful musical monk. "I am music," he says. Playing it is his greatest and perhaps only pleasure. But he's been an ascetic even on that front as of late, recording less than ever, waiting four years between albums. It'll stand as the longest break of his career.

• • •

Prince famously liberated himself from his record deal with Warner Bros. in 1996, and it apparently took him years to realize that his freedom extended to not releasing music. "I write more than I record now, and I also play live a lot more than I record," he says. "I used to record something every day. I always tease that I have to go to studio rehab.

"I'm a very in-the-moment person," he continues. "I do what feels good in the moment . . . I'm not on a schedule, and I don't have any sort of contractual ties. I don't know in history if there's been any musicians that have been self-sufficient like that, not beholden. I have giant bills, large payrolls, so I do have to do tours . . . but there's no need to record anymore." He makes a direct connection between fasting, celibacy, and his abstention from recording. "After four days, you don't want food anymore . . . It's like this thing that says, 'Feed me, feed me.' When it realizes it's not going to get fed, it goes away . . . It's the same with music. I had to see what it's like to stop making albums. And then you go, 'Oh, wait a minute, I don't feel the need to do that anymore.'"

Prince brings me up to the office to play tracks from *Plectrum-Electrum*, the album that would finally break his recording fast. He chose from 100 or so songs laid down in one of the downstairs studios with his recently formed backing band, 3rdEyeGirl—the hardest-rocking ensemble he ever assembled. "All recorded live, no punch-ins," he says. "You just do it till you get the take you like." (The album doesn't come out for another eight months, by which time it's accompanied by a more traditional Prince LP called *Art Official Age*.)

Prince and I meet for the first time a few minutes earlier, as he emerges from a rehearsal space with the young women of the band. Hannah Welton, the drummer, a bubbly twenty-three-year-old who looks like Carrie Underwood and plays like John Bonham, introduces herself brightly: "Hi, I'm Hannah!" Prince laughs, not unkindly, and imitates her, chirping "Hi, I'm Prince" in a high voice, as he reaches out a firm, businesslike handshake. His actual speaking voice is deep, soft and calming, like a DJ on a smooth-jazz station.

As we walk along, he shows no sign of reported double-hip-replacement-surgery—no limp, no cane, no apparent discomfort. His brown eyes are alert, and his wit is quick—looking back, it's nearly impossible to square his affect with posthumous rumors of an opioid addiction. He claims not to feel the passage of time, and says mortality doesn't enter his thoughts: "I don't think about 'gone.'" To the contrary, he is immersed in the moment, invested in a creative future that he believes will be long and bright. The pause between albums seems to have been healthy for him, as is the youthful, enthusiastic, near-worshipful presence of the 3rdEyeGirl members. For the first time in years, he's been opening up Paisley Park to local fans for spontaneous events. There's talk of staging one of these shows on the night of my visit, though it evaporates with no notice.

On his way upstairs, Prince struts past a hallway decorated with a photographic timeline of his career—there's "Batdance" Prince, "Slave"-on-his-face Prince, and even his 1985 *Rolling*

Stone cover (he notes that he refused to do a photo shoot, so we ran a still from a video that, in his considered opinion, made his teeth look strange). "There's room for *Purple Rain* or the Super Bowl here," he notes of one empty space, murmuring something about eventually turning Paisley Park into a museum. It already seems a bit like one: a huge, dark, nearly empty space with only a skeleton crew on hand.

We stop at a mural where a painted image of Prince, arms spread, stands astride images of his influences and artists he, in turn, influenced. He tests me, making sure I can recognize Chaka Khan and Sly and the Family Stone, while giving me a pass on missing Tower of Power and Grand Funk Railroad.

Playing the album in his office, he charmingly takes pains to turn the player's visualizer function on, providing state-of-2002 fractal accompaniment to the music. On a stand in the corner is a century-old Portuguese guitar with a teardrop-shape body. A Canon telephoto lens with no camera attached sits atop a couple of coffee-table books: *Vanity Fair's Hollywood*; *Palaces of Naples*. The walls of the office are painted in a blue-skies motif, with the words "Dream Style" on one of them. Hanging on another wall is a clock emblazoned with the cover of his 2007 album *Planet Earth*—the only timepiece of any kind I see anywhere in Paisley Park.

Between songs, Prince laments the state of a music industry he thinks is focused on anything but music. "You're trying to find the personality first, make sure you've got that locked in," he says. "And it's better if they got scandal on 'em or a reality show or sex tape. And they have it down to an art. They're getting street cred for Justin Bieber now!"

He puts on one of the album's poppier tracks, the sweet throwback "Stopthistrain," with vocals from 3rdEyeGirl drummer Welton and her husband, Josh. I suggest, gently, that the song might fare best on the charts if no one knows of its Prince connection. He nods. "That's kind of the blessing and a curse these days," he says, "that I'm competing with [my] older music. And I don't know anybody who has to do that. They always play Beyoncé's latest track. But I go on Oprah and they want me to play what they remember."

He ends by previewing a couple of songs from what will become *Art Official Age*, excusing himself from the room when he gets to the wailing ballad "Breakdown." The breakup-themed lyrics seem particularly personal: "I used to throw the party every New Year's Eve/First one intoxicated, last one to leave/Waking up in places that you would never believe/Give me back the time, you can keep the memories." Afterward, he confirms that the song comes from a "sensitive . . . nude" place: "You could touch it and it would just hurt instantly."

Before Prince sits for an interview, there is another test. I sit and chat with the members of 3rdEyeGirl in a cavernous atrium, where the black carpet is decorated with Prince's old symbol and the words "NPG Music Club," and the motorcycle from *Purple Rain* is on display above. We gather on a purple couch that is noticeably frayed, and they explain their unlikely origins. The bassist, taciturn Denmark native Ida Nielsen, arrived first, joining Prince's bigger funk band, the latest incarnation of the New Power Generation, which he's still gigging with as well. Prince tells me how she beat out an old bandmate of his who re-auditioned: "She was eight times better than him, and she was new."

Prince specifically wanted a female band, seeking out members via YouTube—back in 2010, he had discovered Nielsen on MySpace. "We're in the feminine aspect now," he says. "That's where society is. You're gonna get a woman president soon. Men have gone as far as they can, right? . . . I learn from women a lot quicker than I do from men . . . At a certain point, you're supposed to know what it means to be a man, but now what do you know about what it means to be a woman? Do you know how to listen? Most men don't know how to listen."

I ask 3rdEyeGirl's guitarist, Donna Grantis, who has a half-shaved head and Hendrixian chops, about her influences. "Prince," she says, flatly. Her husband, a pleasant rocker dude named Trevor Guy, came along with her and ended up working closely with Prince, serving some managerial functions. (Prince believes artists shouldn't have managers: "You should be a grown man, be able to *man*-age yourself.") Josh, Welton's husband, an R&B-singer-turned-producer, also became part of the Paisley family, working on some of Prince's final albums. They've all been living in a nearby hotel for a year and a half, spending at least six days a week in Paisley Park. They come off as members of a benign cult. "It's sort of like an alternate reality," says Grantis. "It's an alternate universe being here, because we're in this awesome bubble of, like, making music all day. I have no idea what the date is or what day it is."

As we talk, I glance over my shoulder and realize that Prince has at some point materialized behind me, silently eavesdropping. He nods and moves away again into the darkness. The band and I go into the industrial kitchen, where we're served dinner, and I am soon summoned into the control room of the complex's Studio A, where Prince sits at the mixing desk. "This room was built in '87, and the first record I did in here was *Lovesexy*," he says. "We never really got this room clickin' like any of my home studios or the hot-rodded boards I used in Los Angeles when I had a record deal. It's real cozy and private—I just kinda wished it sounded like what goes on in my head. And I've been tinkering with things forever . . . I suppose I will keep messing with it—or another generation will."

We talk of many things, and his ban on discussing the past turns out to be slightly flexible. He makes a point of noting that his reputation as the puppet master behind the Time and even Vanity 6 was exaggerated. "It was all collaborative," he says. "It's not just my vision. It's one thing to say, 'You know what would be cool?' and visualize it . . . but then you've got to actually find the people. [The Time's] Morris Day is as good as any funk drummer who ever did it. And Vanity? Nobody could talk like her." He's most passionate and lucid when he talks about music: "'Rock Steady' by Aretha Franklin, 'Cold Sweat' by James [Brown], all the Stax records, Ike and Tina Turner—we took it for granted, thinking that music would always be like that. That was just normal to us."

There are frequent, sometimes tricky-to-follow digressions: He seems to have branched out from his study of the Bible, which began in earnest when he became a Jehovah's Witness under the tutelage of bassist Larry Graham. "It's just all expanded," he says. "Anything I believed then, I believe even more now—it's just expanded." While still deeply Christian, he's also spent time studying what appears to be an Afrocentric interpretation of history, along with the physics of sound, some Eastern ideas (chakras are "science," he says), and a selection of unabashed conspiracy theories. He has thoughts on the JFK assassination ("The car slows down—why doesn't it speed up?"); AIDS ("It's rising in some communities, and it's not rising in others—any primate could figure out why"); and the airplane trails known in some circles as chemtrails ("Think about where they appear, why they appear, how often and what particular times of the year").

At one point, the phone rings: It's the young British singer-songwriter Delilah. Prince's voice suddenly gets even deeper. "I know it's late there," he purrs into the handset. "I'm going to will you awake." On a possibly related note, Prince says he's unsure if he'll marry again. "That's another thing that's up to God," he says. "It's all magnetism anyway—something would pull me into its gravity, and I wouldn't be able to get out from it."

We take a break and head to Paisley Park's empty nightclub, where 3rdEyeGirl are waiting onstage. "I can take you out there and hit this guitar for you," Prince promised earlier, "and what you'll hear is sex. You will hear something where you'd run out of adjectives, like you do when you meet the finest woman." He wants to prove that 3rdEyeGirl can activate my chakras, so he seats me on a stool onstage, no more than three feet away from him. He picks up a custom Vox guitar—the brand some of James Brown's guitarists played. "You're gonna start vibrating in a second," he tells me, and kicks the band into the fiery seventies fusion instrumental "Stratus," tearing through solos that arc endlessly upward. He warned of goose bumps, and delivers.

Afterward, the band does a photo shoot in Studio C— one shot is intended for the cover of a "Stopthistrain" single that never actually comes out. Prince disappears for a while before returning with a MacBook that has Delilah live on Skype—he shows her the shoot via webcam. It's past midnight when we begin talking again. He mentions a desire to mentor Chris Brown, says he invited him to Paisley Park. I note that some people think what Brown did to Rihanna was unforgivable. He's shocked. "Unforgivable?" he says. "Goodness. That's when we go check the master, Christ . . . Have you ever instantly forgiven somebody?" I shake my head. "It's the best feeling in the world, and it totally dismantles that person's whole stance."

He talks more about mentoring and helping peers, so I wonder aloud if he thinks he could've forestalled Michael Jackson's fate. "I don't want to talk about it," Prince says at first. "I'm too close to it." He goes on: "He is just one of many who have gone through that door—Amy Winehouse and folks. We're all connected, right, we're all brothers and sisters, and the minute we lock that in, we wouldn't let anybody in our family fall. That's why I called Chris Brown. All of us need to be able to reach out and just fix stuff. There's nothing that's unforgivable."

He seems to be hinting at past problems of his own, so I ask if he was ever self-destructive. His eyebrows shoot up. "Self-destructive? I mean . . . do I look self-destructive?" This leads him to a disquisition on why he avoids talking about the past. "People say, 'Why did you change your name?' and this, that, and the other. I'm here right now, doing what I'm doing right now, and all of the things I did led up to this. And there is no place else I'd rather be than right now. I want to be talking to you, and I want you to get it."

We talk about retirement. "I don't know what that is," he says. "There's always some way to serve . . . It feels like I'm teaching at a school, but also a student at one. I never felt like I had a job—does that make sense? So those words, 'job' and 'retire' . . ."

He tries to explain why he can imagine playing into old age, with a dizzying detour into mysticism via the Wachowskis. "Life spans are getting longer," he says. "One of the reasons is because people are learning more about everything, so then the brain makes more connections. Eventually, we'll be in eternal brain mode because we'll be able to hold eternity in our minds. A lot of people can't do that. If you can't think all the way back eternally, you can't think all the way forward eternally. Everybody usually thinks about a beginning, a big bang. If you take that event out, then you can start to see what eternity is. Remember in *The Matrix* where they said the only thing that has an ending had a beginning, and vice versa?"

It's nearly 2:00 a.m., and Prince is done for the night. He walks me through the depths of Paisley Park, his shoes glowing in the dark, to retrieve my jacket and bag. As we walk, I hear doves cry—actual doves that live in a cage somewhere in the rafters. As I put on my coat, Prince invites me to join the band in London. The zipper catches badly on the way up. "Fuck," I say, and my host looks stricken.

"So much for not cursing," he says.

I apologize. Prince looks me in the eyes, and wraps me in a tight hug. I am, as promised, dismantled by his instant forgiveness. I can still feel that embrace as I walk outside, where moonlight shines on a thick layer of immaculate, freshly fallen snow.

"TRANSCENDENCE. THAT'S WHAT YOU WANT. WHEN THAT HAPPENS—OH, BOY"

INTERVIEW WITH ALEXIS PETRIDIS
THE GUARDIAN
NOVEMBER 2015

When our correspondent was abruptly summoned to an audience with the legendary artist in his Minneapolis studios, he had no idea what to expect. Certainly not being asked to duet on *Sign O' the Times* . . .

In 1985, Prince released a single called "Paisley Park," the first to be taken from his psychedelic opus, *Around the World In a Day*. It's one of several Prince songs that describe a location that's a kind of mystical utopia.

Paisley Park, the lyrics aver, is filled with laughing children on seesaws and "colorful people" with expressions that "speak of profound inner peace," whatever they look like. "Love is the color this place imparts," it continues. "There aren't any rules in Paisley Park."

It's all a bit difficult to square with Paisley Park, the vast studio complex Prince built a couple of years later. It sits behind a chain-link fence in the nondescript Minnesota suburb of Chanhassen, and there's no getting around the fact that, from the outside at least, it looks less like a mystical utopia, more like a branch of Ikea.

Inside, however, it looks almost exactly like you'd imagine a huge recording complex owned by Prince would look. There is a lot of purple. The symbol that represented Prince's name for most of the nineties is everywhere: hanging from the ceiling, painted on speakers and the studio's mixing desks, illuminating one room in the form of a neon sign.

There is something called the Galaxy Room, apparently intended for meditation: it is illuminated entirely by ultra-violet lights and has paintings of planets on the walls. There are murals depicting the studio's owner, never a man exactly crippled by modesty.

And there are two full-sized live-music venues: a vast, hangar-like space that also features a food concession—form an orderly queue for Funky House Party In Your Mouth Cheesecake ($4)—and a smaller room decked out to look like a nightclub. I am currently on the stage of the latter, along with four other representatives of the European press.

We are literally sitting at Prince's feet: feet, it's perhaps worth noting, that are wearing a pair of flip-flops with huge platform soles teamed with socks. The socks and flip-flops are white, as is the rest of his outfit: skinny flared trousers, a T-shirt with long sleeves, also flared. As skinny as a teen-ager, sporting an afro and almost unnecessarily handsome at fifty-seven years old, Prince looks flatly amazing—exuding ineffable cool and panache while wearing clothes that would make anyone else look like a ninny is just one among his panoply of talents.

We are seated at his feet because we are supposed to be asking Prince questions: we've been summoned to Paisley Park at short notice, apparently because Prince "had a brainstorm in the middle of the night, two nights ago" and decided this was the best way to announce a forthcoming European tour.

First, there was a tour of the studio accompanied by Trevor Guy, who works for Prince's record label NPG: he's friendly, effusive about his boss's talents and a little evasive when someone asks him whereabouts in Minneapolis Prince actually lives. ("He doesn't live here. I don't know where he lives.")

Then we were told we were getting a treat, which turned out to be listening to some cover versions Prince's current protege, Andy Allo, recorded with the man himself on guitar. While we're listening to Andy Allo sing Roxy Music's "More Than This," Prince suddenly appears on the stage and beckons us over.

The dates haven't actually been confirmed yet, but the concept has: he's going to perform solo, playing the piano, in a succession of theaters. "Well, I'm not one to get bad reviews," he deadpans.

"So I'm doing it to challenge myself, like tying one hand behind my back, not relying on the craft that I've known for thirty years. I won't know what songs I'm going to do when I go on stage, I really won't. I won't have to, because I won't have a band. Tempo, keys, all those things can dictate what song I'm going to play next, you know, as opposed to, 'Oh, I've got to do my hit single now, I've got to play this album all the way through,' or whatever. There's so much material, it's hard to choose. It's hard. So that's what I'd like to do."

Prince, it has to be said, is proving the very model of softly spoken charm. He's also wryly funny on topics ranging from his songwriting ("I have to do it to clear my head, it's like . . . shaking an Etch A Sketch") to the activist Rachel Dolezal, or as he puts it, "that lady who said she was black even though she was white," to his famous 2010 pronouncement that "the internet is completely over."

"What I meant was that the internet was over for anyone who wants to get paid, and I was right about that," he says.

"Tell me a musician who's got rich off digital sales. Apple's doing pretty good though, right?"

It's all a far cry from the days when he refused to talk to the press, disparaged them in song—"Take a bath, hippies!" he snapped in 1982's "All The Critics Love U In New York"— or dismissed them "mamma-jammas wearing glasses and an alligator shirt behind a typewriter."

"Oh, I love critics," he smiles. "Because they love me. It's not a joke. They care. See, everybody knows when somebody's lazy, and now, with the internet, it's impossible for a writer to be lazy because everybody will pick up on it. In the past, they said some stuff that was out of line, so I just didn't have anything to do with them. Now it gets embarrassing to say something untrue, because you put it online and everyone knows about it, so it's better to tell the truth."

Nevertheless, it's turning out to be harder to ask questions than you might think. Prince is seated at a microphone behind a keyboard, which he keeps playing. This is quite disconcerting: if he doesn't like a question, he strikes up with the theme from *The Twilight Zone* and shakes his head. At one point, he presses a button on the keyboard and the intro to his legendary 1988 hit "Sign O' the Times" booms out of the PA.

He looks at me. "You wanna do this?" he says. I look back at him aghast: there are doubtless things I want to do less than sing Prince's legendary 1988 hit "Sign O' the Times" in front of Prince, but at this exact moment I'm struggling to think of any. For one thing, Prince is, by common consent, the one bona-fide, no-further-questions musical genius that eighties pop produced; a man who can play pretty much any instrument he chooses, possessed of a remarkable voice that can still leap effortlessly from baritone to falsetto.

I, on the other hand, am a deeply unfunky Englishman with no discernible musical ability: the sound of my singing voice can ruin your day. For another, I'm a journalist, and thus aware that among Prince's panoply of talents lies a nonpareil ability to screw with journalists. Rumors abound of him demanding hacks dance in front of him. Only if their gyrations are deemed sufficiently funky do they get face time.

A recent visitor to Paisley Park found himself standing in the studio having a telephone conversation with Prince, who, it later transpired, was standing in the next room all along. The novelist Matt Thorne, author of a 500-page book that stands as the definitive work on Prince's oeuvre, tells a story of pursuing him for an interview, and being invited to attend a gig in New York.

Midway through a guitar solo, Prince spotted Thorne in the audience, walked over, whispered: "How about that interview?" then ran off, still soloing: Thorne never heard from him again. So I shake my head and say no: for a mercy, Prince shrugs and turns the music off and we plough on, albeit a little awkwardly.

Without wishing to bore you with the mechanics of interview technique, it's hard to get a conversational beat going—or indeed to chase up answers that seem evasive or tangential to the actual question—when there are four other people there, eager to have their say, among them a man who appears to have traveled from France with the specific intention of not asking any questions, but simply impressing on Prince how many times he's seen him live, and an

Italian journalist keen to know how the artist's latter-day religious beliefs affected what he insists on referring to as his "Sex Issues."

The latter is actually a fair question: few artists in history have had musical Sex Issues on quite the scale that Prince did. Incest ("Sister"), references to rape ("Lust U Always"), a queasy description of his first sexual partner's vagina ("Schoolyard"): before becoming a Jehovah's Witness, Prince once considered this all fair game in his concerted effort to shock.

It would be intriguing to know where he draws the line now—among the covers he and Andy Allo recorded was an old song of his, "I Love U in Me," which is hardly Sunday school fare, while a journalist invited to Paisley Park to hear his recent album *Plectrumelectrum* was startled to see Prince run from the room when a particularly spicy lyric he'd "forgotten about" blared from the speakers—but his answer is a little vague. "It just makes me think more in terms of detail.

Could I say things better, more succinctly, more truly? And wider, for example, if you want kids to come to your concerts. Now I've got older fans, they have families, so they want to bring their kids, so I think it's a pretty good move to take some of those songs out, so you can get a bigger audience, to experience the same thing."

No, he says, he never considered just changing the lyrics of a beloved but filthy old song like "Head" or "Darling Nikki" so that he could still perform it. "You want to hear it? It's on an album. I write so many songs that I don't even think about those songs anymore. I don't get attached to it. Because if I did, I couldn't move on and there'd be no space for a new song like 'Stare.' That's what you want to listen to."

The subject that really gets him going is his famous bête noir, the music industry. He's dallied with a number of record labels since his legendary nineties dispute with Warner Bros., but he's still given to describing record-business contracts as "slavery," protesting that the industry gives black artists a rough deal—"I think history speaks for itself. You know, U2 don't have a problem with their label. They love their record label"—and advising new artists not to sign anything.

"Larry King asked me once, didn't you need a record company to make it [in the music business]? But that has nothing to do with it. I was well known starting out, we had a great band and every time we played, we got better. We also had studio work, so the more we recorded the better we got. This is what you've got to do, and if you've got great folk around you and a good teacher, you're going to excel at it.

"You don't need a record company to turn you into anything. It wasn't like they were directing our flow whatsoever, you know. I had autonomous control from the very beginning to make my album."

He says there's no danger in modern music: "When was the last time you were scared by anyone? In the seventies, there was scary stuff then." He suggests that the blame for any malaise lies not merely with the record companies— "accountants and lawyers stepped in while producers were in the studio, they started looking for things that they thought would work, so dozens of rock bands come out every week and you can't even name them"—but also a lack of jazz-fusion bands. The latter, you have to say, seems a fairly unique interpretation of the situation.

"Well, I don't think people learn technique anymore. There are no great jazz-fusion bands. I grew up seeing Weather Report, and I don't see anything remotely like that now. There's nothing to copy from, because you can't go and see a band like Weather Report. Al Di Meola, the guitar player, he'd just stand in the center of the stage, soloing, until everyone gives him a standing ovation. Those were the memories that I grew up with and that made me want to play."

He's keen to emphasize that it's an urge that's never left him. Last night, he says, he sat here alone, after everyone else had gone home, and played and sang for three hours straight. "I just couldn't stop," he says. He'd got "in the zone . . . like an out-of-body experience": it felt like he was sitting in the audience watching himself. "That's what you want. Transcendence. When that happens"—he shakes his head—"Oh, boy."

Still, it seems an oddly lonely image: sitting in an empty building in the middle of nowhere in the small hours. It makes me think of a heartbreaking interview he gave to *Rolling Stone* in the mid-eighties, when he was clearly struggling to come to terms with the isolating effects of global superstardom.

He invited the writer back to his house and confided that his then-girlfriend had offered to show up while the journalist was there "to make it seem like you have friends come by," but Prince had declined because "that would be lying." I ask if there's anything he still misses from the years before he became one of the biggest stars in the world.

"No," he says firmly. "These days, I can get more done. I'm far more respected than I was before, when I say something with regard to changes in the music industry." And then he changes the subject to Jay-Z's streaming service Tidal, with which Prince has recently signed, and draws the interview to a close: "Are we good?"

Later that night, he's back on the stage again, playing one of the regular secret Paisley Park shows that locals pay $40 to attend, unaware of whether Prince will actually perform or not. I sit next to a mother and daughter who have turned up on three occasions: the only previous glimpse they got of Prince was spotting him riding a bicycle around the car park, which I suppose is a sight worth seeing in itself.

When he sits back at the piano and plays "Raspberry Beret" and "Starfish and Coffee" and "Girls and Boys," they're beside themselves, and understandably so: he sounds magnificent. He plays covers of songs by of the Staples Singers and Chaka Khan, and a couple of funk jams with his band.

Then he invites the audience to come to the cinema and watch the new James Bond film with him, and vanishes before anyone can try take him up on the offer: presumably he's gone home, wherever that is.

PRINCE ROGERS NELSON (1958–2016) was a musician, performer, and filmmaker. One of the most acclaimed and bestselling artists of the twentieth century, Prince was born to musician parents and raised in Minneapolis, where he would remain for most of his life. His signature sound, an innovative blend of popular musical styles that incorporated elements of funk, rock, R&B, soul, and new wave, influenced and was emulated by countless musicians.

LISA CRAWFORD attended Minnesota's Central High School with Prince.

LISA HENDRIKSSON formerly reported on music and culture for the *Minnesota Daily*.

ANDY SCHWARTZ served as the editor and publisher of *New York Rocker* until it ceased print publication in 1982. From 1989 to 2000 he served as the director of editorial services at Epic Records.

STEVE FARGNOLI was Prince's manager from 1979–1989. Fargnoli later managed Sinéad O'Connor until his death in 2001.

ADRIAN DEEVOY has written since 1978 for a variety of music publications including *Trouser Press*, *International Musician*, *Penthouse*, *Cosmopolitan*, *Q Magazine*, *GQ*, *The Times* [London], the *Los Angeles Times*, *The Sunday Times*, *Blender*, *Le Monde*, *Der Spiegel*, *The Times of India*, and *The Observer*. In addition to Prince, Deevoy has interviewed Bob Dylan, Prince, Madonna, and Freddie Mercury.

CATHERINE CENSOR (passé **SHEMO)** is a writer, editor, and a former managing editor of *Vegetarian Times*.

BEN GREENMAN is a novelist, magazine journalist, and a former editor for *The New Yorker*. He is the author of several books, including the novel *The Slippage* and the essay collection *Emotional Rescue*. He has also coauthored the memoirs of musicians such as Questlove, George Clinton, and Brian Wilson.

CLAIRE HOFFMAN is an American journalist, author, and assistant professor of journalism at the University of California, Riverside. She is the author of the memoir *Greetings from Utopia Park: Surviving a Transcendental Childhood*.

BRIAN HIATT is a senior writer at *Rolling Stone*, where he also hosts the podcast *Rolling Stone Music Now*. Hiatt is also the editor of *A Portrait of Bowie: A Tribute to Bowie by His Artistic collaborators and contemporaries*.

ALEXIS PETRIDIS is *The Guardian*'s rock and pop critic.

THE LAST INTERVIEW SERIES

KURT VONNEGUT: THE LAST INTERVIEW

"I think it can be tremendously refreshing if a creator of literature has something on his mind other than the history of literature so far. Literature should not disappear up its own asshole, so to speak."

$15.95 / $17.95 CAN
978-1-61219-090-7
ebook: 978-1-61219-091-4

JACQUES DERRIDA: THE LAST INTERVIEW
LEARNING TO LIVE FINALLY

"I am at war with myself, it's true, you couldn't possibly know to what extent... I say contradictory things that are, we might say, in real tension; they are what construct me, make me live, and will make me die."

translated by PASCAL-ANNE BRAULT and MICHAEL NAAS

$15.95 / $17.95 CAN
978-1-61219-094-5
ebook: 978-1-61219-032-7

ROBERTO BOLAÑO: THE LAST INTERVIEW

"Posthumous: It sounds like the name of a Roman gladiator, an unconquered gladiator. At least that's what poor Posthumous would like to believe. It gives him courage."

translated by SYBIL PEREZ and others

$15.95 / $17.95 CAN
978-1-61219-095-2
ebook: 978-1-61219-033-4

THE LAST INTERVIEW SERIES

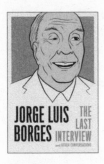

JORGE LUIS BORGES: THE LAST INTERVIEW

"Believe me: the benefits of blindness have been greatly exaggerated. If I could see, I would never leave the house, I'd stay indoors reading the many books that surround me."

translated by KIT MAUDE

$15.95 / $15.95 CAN
978-1-61219-204-8
ebook: 978-1-61219-205-5

HANNAH ARENDT: THE LAST INTERVIEW

"There are no dangerous thoughts for the simple reason that thinking itself is such a dangerous enterprise."

$15.95 / $15.95 CAN
978-1-61219-311-3
ebook: 978-1-61219-312-0

RAY BRADBURY: THE LAST INTERVIEW

"You don't have to destroy books to destroy a culture. Just get people to stop reading them."

$15.95 / $15.95 CAN
978-1-61219-421-9
ebook: 978-1-61219-422-6

THE LAST INTERVIEW SERIES

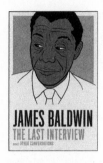

JAMES BALDWIN: THE LAST INTERVIEW

"You don't realize that you're intelligent until it gets you into trouble."

$15.95 / $15.95 CAN
978-1-61219-400-4
ebook: 978-1-61219-401-1

GABRIEL GÁRCIA MÁRQUEZ: THE LAST INTERVIEW

"The only thing the Nobel Prize is good for is not having to wait in line."

$15.95 / $15.95 CAN
978-1-61219-480-6
ebook: 978-1-61219-481-3

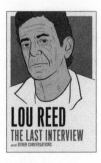

LOU REED: THE LAST INTERVIEW

"Hubert Selby. William Burroughs. Allen Ginsberg. Delmore Schwartz... I thought if you could do what those writers did and put it to drums and guitar, you'd have the greatest thing on earth."

$15.95 / $15.95 CAN
978-1-61219-478-3
ebook: 978-1-61219-479-0

THE LAST INTERVIEW SERIES

ERNEST HEMINGWAY: THE LAST INTERVIEW

"The most essential gift for a good writer is a
built-in, shockproof shit detector."

$15.95 / $20.95 CAN
978-1-61219-522-3
ebook: 978-1-61219-523-0

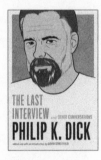

PHILIP K. DICK: THE LAST INTERVIEW

"The basic thing is, how frightened are you of
chaos? And how happy are you with order?"

$15.95 / $20.95 CAN
978-1-61219-526-1
ebook: 978-1-61219-527-8

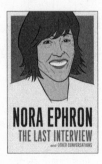

NORA EPHRON: THE LAST INTERVIEW

"You better *make* them care about what you think.
It had better be quirky or perverse or thought-
ful enough so that you hit some chord in them.
Otherwise, it doesn't work."

$15.95 / $20.95 CAN
978-1-61219-524-7
ebook: 978-1-61219-525-4

THE LAST INTERVIEW SERIES

JANE JACOBS: THE LAST INTERVIEW

"I would like it to be understood that all our human economic achievements have been done by ordinary people, not by exceptionally educated people, or by elites, or by supernatural forces."

$15.95 / $20.95 CAN
978-1-61219-534-6
ebook: 978-1-61219-535-3

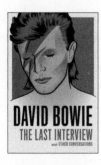

DAVID BOWIE: THE LAST INTERVIEW

"I have no time for glamour. It seems a ridiculous thing to strive for . . . A clean pair of shoes should serve quite well."

$16.99 / $22.99 CAN
978-1-61219-575-9
ebook: 978-1-61219-576-6

MARTIN LUTHER KING, JR.: THE LAST INTERVIEW

"Injustice anywhere is a threat to justice everywhere."

$15.99 / $21.99 CAN
978-1-61219-616-9
ebook: 978-1-61219-617-6

THE LAST INTERVIEW SERIES

CHRISTOPHER HITCHENS: THE LAST INTERVIEW

"If someone says I'm doing this out of faith, I say, Why don't you do it out of conviction?"

$15.99 / $20.99 CAN
978-1-61219-672-5
ebook: 978-1-61219-673-2

HUNTER S. THOMPSON: THE LAST INTERVIEW

"I feel in the mood to write a long weird story—a tale so strange and terrible that it will change the brain of the normal reader forever."

$15.99 / $20.99 CAN
978-1-61219-693-0
ebook: 978-1-61219-694-7

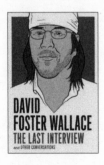

DAVID FOSTER WALLACE: THE LAST INTERVIEW AND OTHER CONVERSATIONS

"I'm a typical American. Half of me is dying to give myself away, and the other half is continually rebelling."

$16.99 / 21.99 CAN
978-1-61219-741-8
ebook: 978-1-61219-742-5

THE LAST INTERVIEW SERIES

KATHY ACKER: THE LAST INTERVIEW AND OTHER CONVERSATIONS

"To my mind I was in a little cage in the zoo that instead of 'monkey' said 'female American radical.'"

$15.99 / $20.99 CAN
978-1-61219-731-9
ebook: 978-1-61219-732-6